Introduction to Dependent Types with Idris

Encoding Program Proofs in Types

Boro Sitnikovski

Apress®

Introduction to Dependent Types with Idris: Encoding Program Proofs in Types

Boro Sitnikovski
Skopje, North Macedonia

ISBN-13 (pbk): 978-1-4842-9258-7 · ISBN-13 (electronic): 978-1-4842-9259-4
https://doi.org/10.1007/978-1-4842-9259-4

Copyright © 2023 by Boro Sitnikovski

Managing Director, Apress Media LLC: Welmoed Spahr
Acquisitions Editor: Celestin Suresh John
Development Editor: James Markham
Coordinating Editor: Mark Powers
Copy Editor: Kezia Endsley

Cover designed by eStudioCalamar
Cover image by Stephanie Mulrooney on Unsplash (www.unsplash.com)

Distributed to the book trade worldwide by Apress Media, LLC, 1 New York Plaza, New York, NY 10004, U.S.A. Phone 1-800-SPRINGER, fax (201) 348-4505, e-mail orders-ny@springer-sbm.com, or visit www.springeronline.com. Apress Media, LLC is a California LLC and the sole member (owner) is Springer Science + Business Media Finance Inc (SSBM Finance Inc). SSBM Finance Inc is a **Delaware** corporation.

For information on translations, please e-mail booktranslations@springernature.com; for reprint, paperback, or audio rights, please e-mail bookpermissions@springernature.com.

Apress titles may be purchased in bulk for academic, corporate, or promotional use. eBook versions and licenses are also available for most titles. For more information, reference our Print and eBook Bulk Sales web page at http://www.apress.com/bulk-sales.

Any source code or other supplementary material referenced by the author in this book is available to readers on GitHub (https://github.com/Apress). For more detailed information, please visit http://www.apress.com/source-code.

Printed on acid-free paper

Dedicated to my wife Dijana and our kids

Table of Contents

About the Author

Boro Sitnikovski has over ten years of experience working professionally as a software engineer. He started programming using the Assembly programming language on an Intel x86 at the age of ten. While in high school, he won several prizes for competitive programming.

He is an informatics graduate; his bachelor's thesis was titled "Programming in Haskell Using Algebraic Data Structures," and his master's thesis was titled "Formal Verification of Instruction Sets in Virtual Machines." He has also published papers on software verification. Other research interests include programming languages, mathematics, logic, algorithms, and writing correct software.

He is a strong believer in the open-source philosophy and contributes to various open-source projects.

In his spare time, he enjoys time with his family.

About the Technical Reviewers

Nathan Bloomfield holds a PhD in algebra from the University of Arkansas and taught mathematics before joining Automattic, Inc. as a programmer. He enjoys witnessing the intuitionist renaissance and likes how the boring parts of abstract algebra transform into really interesting computer science. Nathan usually feels a little out of his depth and prefers it that way.

Neil Mitchell is a Haskell programmer with a PhD in Computer Science from York University, where he worked on making functional programs shorter, faster, and safer. Neil is the author of popular Haskell tools such as Hoogle, HLint, and Ghcid—all designed to help developers write good code quickly. More recently, Neil has been researching build systems with publications at ICFP and the Haskell Symposium, and a practical system based on those ideas named Shake.

Marin Nikolovski works at Massive Entertainment | A Ubisoft Studio as a senior web developer on UPlay PC. He has over ten years of experience designing, developing, and testing software across a variety of platforms. He takes pride in coding to consistently high standards and constantly tries to keep up with the latest developments in the IT industry.

Vlad Riscutia is a software engineer at Microsoft working on Office. He is interested in programming languages and type systems, and how these can best be leveraged to write correct code.

Acknowledgments

Special thanks to the Haskell community (#haskell@freenode), the Idris community (#idris@freenode), and the Coq community (#coq@freenode).

Thanks to my family, coworkers, and friends for all the support they give me.

Finally, thank you for purchasing this book! I hope that you will learn new techniques in reading this book and that it will spark interest in logic, dependent types, and type theory.

Preface

This book aims to be accessible to novices who have no prior experience beyond high school mathematics. Thus, this book is designed to be self-contained. No programming experience is assumed. However, having some kind of programming experience with the functional programming paradigm will make things easier to grasp in the beginning. After you finish reading the book, I recommend that you check the "Further Reading" section if you are interested in diving deeper into some of the topics discussed.

I have always been curious about understanding how things work. As a result, I became very interested in mathematics while I was in high school. One of the reasons for writing this book is that I could not find a book that explained how things work, so I had to do a lot of research on the Internet through white papers, forums, and example code in order to come up with a complete picture of what dependent types are and what they are good for.

I will consider this book successful if it provides you with some additional knowledge. I tried to write this book so that the definitions and examples provided in it show how different pieces of the puzzle are connected.

Feel free to contact me at `buritomath@gmail.com` for any questions you might have, and I will do my best to answer. You can also access my blog at `boro.wordpress.com` to check out some of my latest work.

Introduction

Writing correct code in software engineering is a complex and expensive task, and too often our written code produces inaccurate or unexpected results. There are several ways to deal with this problem. In practice, the most common approach is to write tests, which means that you are writing more code to test your original code. However, these tests can only detect problems in specific cases. As Edsger Dijkstra noted, "testing shows the presence, not the absence of bugs." A less common approach is to find a proof of correctness for your code. A software proof of correctness is a logical proof that the software is functioning according to given specifications. With valid proofs, you can cover all possible cases and be more confident that the code does exactly what it was intended to do.

Idris is a general-purpose functional[1] programming language that supports dependent types. The features of Idris are influenced by Haskell, another general-purpose functional programming language. Thus, Idris shares many features with Haskell, especially in the part of syntax and types, where Idris has a more advanced type system. There are several other programming languages that support dependent types[2]; however, I chose Idris for its readable syntax.

The first version of Idris was released in 2009. It is developed by The Idris Community and led by Dr. Edwin Brady. Seen as a programming language, it is a functional programming language implemented with dependent types. Seen as a logical system, it implements intuitionistic type theory, which I cover later. Finally, Chapter 4 shows how these two views relate.

---

[1] The core concept of functional programming languages is a mathematical function.

[2] Several other languages with dependent types support are Coq, Agda, Lean.

Idris allows you to express mathematical statements. By mechanically examining these statements, it helps you find a formal proof of a program's formal specification.

To fully explain how proofs in Idris work, the book starts with the foundations by defining formal systems, classical mathematical logic, lambda calculus, intuitionistic logic, and type theory (which is a more "up-to-date" version of classical mathematical logic).

CHAPTER 1

Formal Systems

Before you can construct proofs of correctness for software, you need to understand what a proof is and what it means for a proof to be valid. This is the role of *formal systems*. The purpose of formal systems is to let you reason about reasoning—to manipulate logical proofs in terms of their *form*, rather than their *content*. This level of abstraction makes formal systems powerful tools.

Definition 1   A **formal system** is a model of abstract reasoning. A formal system consists of:

1. A **formal language** that contains:

    1. A finite set of *symbols*, which can be combined into finite strings called *formulas*.

    2. *Grammar*, which are rules that tell which formulas are "well-formed."

2. A set of **axioms**, which are formulas that we accept as "valid" without justification.

3. A set of **inference rules,** which tell us how we can derive new, valid formulas from old ones.

© Boro Sitnikovski 2023
B. Sitnikovski, *Introduction to Dependent Types with Idris*,
https://doi.org/10.1007/978-1-4842-9259-4_1

Inside a given formal system, the grammar determines which formulas are *syntactically* sensible, while the inference rules govern which formulas are *semantically* sensible. The difference between these two is important. For example, if the English language is a (very complicated!) formal system, the sentence "Colorless green ideas sleep furiously" is syntactically valid (since different parts of speech are used in the right places), but is semantically nonsense.

After a formal system is defined, other formal systems can extend it. For example, set theory is based on first-order logic, which is based on propositional logic that represents a formal system. The next chapter briefly covers this theory.

ⓘ Definition 2   For a given formal system, a system is **incomplete** if there are statements that are true but cannot be proven to be true inside that system. Conversely, a system is **complete** if all true statements can be proven.

The statement, "This statement is not provable" can either be true or false. When it is true, it is not provable. Alternatively, when it is false, it is provable, but you're trying to prove something false. Thus, the system is incomplete, because some truths are unprovable.

ⓘ Definition 3   For a given formal system, a system is **inconsistent** if there is a theorem in that system that is contradictory. Conversely, a system is **consistent** if there are no contradictory theorems.

A simple example is the statement, "This statement is false". This statement is true if and only if[1] it is false, and therefore it is neither true nor false.

In general, we often focus on which parts of mathematics can be formalized in concrete formal systems, rather than trying to find a theory in which all mathematics can be developed. The reason for that is Gödel's incompleteness theorem. This theorem states that there doesn't exist[2] a formal system that is both complete and consistent. As a result, it is better to reason about a formal system outside of the system (at the meta-language level), since the object level (rules within the system) can be limiting. The famous saying says to "think outside of the box," which is how we sometimes do meta-thinking to improve ourselves.

In conclusion, formal systems are an attempt to abstract models whenever we reverse-engineer nature in an attempt to understand it better. They may be imperfect but are nevertheless useful tools for reasoning.

1.1. MU Puzzle Example

The MU puzzle is a formal system that's used as an example in this section.

---

[1] The word iff is an abbreviation for "If and only if" and means that two statements are logically equivalent.

[2] Note that this theorem only holds for systems that allow expressing arithmetic of natural numbers (e.g., Peano, set theory, but first-order logic also has some paradoxes if you allow self-referential statements). This is because the incompleteness theorem relies on the Gödel numbering concept, which allows a formal system to reason about itself by using symbols in the system to map expressions in that same system. For example, 0 is mapped to 1, S is 2, = is 3, so 0 = S0 $\Longleftrightarrow$ (1, 3, 2, 1). Using this, you can express statements about the system within the system, which are self-referential statements. The next chapter looks into these systems.

ℹ️ **Definition 4**   You're given a starting string, MI, combined with a few inference rules or transformation rules:

No.	Rule	Description	Example
1	xI → xIU	Append U at a string ending in I	MI to MIU
2	Mx → Mxx	Double the string after M	MIU to MIUIU
3	xIIIy → xUy	Replace III inside a string with U	MUIIIU to MUUU
4	xUUy → xy	Remove UU from inside a string	MUUU to MU

In the inference rules, the symbols M, I, and U are part of the system, while x is a variable that stands for any symbol(s). For example, MI matches rule 2 for x = I, and it can also match rule 1 for x = M. Another example is MII, which matches rule 2 for x = II and rule 1 for x = MI.

You will now see how to show (or prove) how to get from MI to MIIU using the inference rules:

1. MI (axiom)
2. MII (rule 2, x = I)
3. MIIII (rule 2, x = II)
4. MIIIIIIII (rule 2, x = IIII)
5. MUIIIII (rule 3, x = M, y = IIIII)
6. MUUII (rule 3, x = MU, y = II)
7. MII (rule 4, x = M, y = II)
8. MIIU (rule 1, x = MI)

You can represent the formal description of this system as follows:

1. Formal language

   1. A set of symbols is {M, I, U }

   2. A string is well-formed if the first letter is M and there are no other M letters. Examples: M, MIUIU, and MUUUIII

2. MI is the starting string, that is, an axiom

3. The rules of inference are defined in Definition 4

 Can you get from MI to MU with this system?

To answer this, you use an invariant[3] with mathematical induction to prove this claim.

To be able to apply Rule 3, you need the number of subsequent Is to be divisible by 3. Let's have the invariant say that, "There is no sequence of Is in the string with a length divisible by 3":

1. For the starting axiom, you have one I. Invariant OK.

2. Applying rule 2 will double the number of Is, so you can have: I, II, IIII, and IIIIIII (in particular, 2^n Is). Invariant OK.

3. Applying rule 3 will reduce the number of Is by 3. But note that 2n - 3 is still not divisible by 3[4]. Invariant OK.

---

[3] An *invariant* is a property that holds whenever you apply any of the inference rules.

[4] After having been introduced to proofs, you will be given an exercise to prove this fact.

You've shown that with the starting axiom MI, it is not possible to get to MU because no sequence of steps can turn a string with one I into a string with no Is. But if you look carefully, this uses a different formal system to reason about MU (i.e., divisibility by 3, which is not part of the MU system). This is because the puzzle cannot be solved in its own system. Otherwise, an algorithm would keep trying different inference rules of MU indefinitely (not knowing that MU is impossible).

Every useful formal system has this limitation. As you've seen, Gödel's theorem shows that there's no formal system that can contain all possible truths, because it cannot prove some truths about its own structure. Thus, having experience with different formal systems and combining them as needed can be useful.

CHAPTER 2

Classical Mathematical Logic

All engineering disciplines involve some logic. The foundations of Idris, as you will see later, are based on a system that implements (or encodes) classical mathematical logic so that you can easily "map" this logic and its inference rules to computer programs.

2.1. Hierarchy of Mathematical Logic and Definitions

At its core, mathematical logic deals with mathematical concepts expressed using formal logical systems. This section looks at the hierarchy of these logical systems. The reason there are different levels of hierarchies is that each level has more power in expressiveness. Further, these logical systems allow you to produce proofs.

© Boro Sitnikovski 2023
B. Sitnikovski, *Introduction to Dependent Types with Idris*,
https://doi.org/10.1007/978-1-4842-9259-4_2

2.1.1. Propositional Logic

ⓘ Definition 1   The propositional branch of logic is concerned with the study of **propositions**, which are statements that are either ⊤ (true) or ⊥ (false). Variables can be used to represent propositions. Propositions are formed by other propositions with the use of logical connectives. The most basic logical connectives are ∧ (and), ∨ (or), ¬ (negation), and → (implication).

For example, you can say a = Salad is organic, and thus the variable a represents a true statement. Another statement is a = Rock is organic, and thus a is a false statement. The statement a = Hi there! is neither a true nor a false statement, and thus is not a proposition.

The "and" connective means that both *a* and *b* have to be true in order for $a \wedge b$ to be true. For example, the statement I like milk and sugar is true as a whole iff (if and only if) both I like milk and I like sugar are true.

a	b	$a \wedge b$
⊤	⊤	⊤
⊤	⊥	⊥
⊥	⊤	⊥
⊥	⊥	⊥

The "or" connective means that either of *a* or *b* has to be true in order for $a \vee b$ to be true. It will also be true if both *a* and *b* are true. This is known as *inclusive or*. For example, the statement I like milk or sugar is true as a whole if at least one of I like milk or I like sugar is true.

This definition of "or" might be a bit counterintuitive to the way we use it in day to day speaking. When we say I like milk or sugar we normally mean one of them but not both. This is known as *exclusive or*. However, for the purposes of this book, we use inclusive or.

a	b	$a \vee b$
T	T	T
T	⊥	T
⊥	T	T
⊥	⊥	⊥

The negation connective simply swaps the truthiness of a proposition. The easiest way to negate any statement is to just prepend It is not the case that ... to it. For example, the negation of I like milk is It is not the case that I like milk, or simply I don't like milk.

a	¬a
T	⊥
⊥	T

The implication connective allows you to express conditional statements, and its interpretation is subtle. We say that $a \rightarrow b$ is true if anytime a is true, it is necessarily also the case that b is true. Another way to think about implication is in terms of *promises*; $a \rightarrow b$ represents a promise that if a happens, then b also happens. In this interpretation, the truth value of $a \rightarrow b$ is whether or not the promise is kept, and we say that a promise is kept unless it has been broken.

For example, if you choose a = Today is your birthday and b = I brought you a cake, then $a \rightarrow b$ represents the promise If today is your birthday, then I brought you a cake. Then there are four ways that today can play out:

- Today is your birthday, and I brought you a cake. The promise is kept, so the implication is true

- Today is your birthday, but I did not bring you a cake. The promise is not kept, so the implication is false

- Today is not your birthday, and I brought you a cake. Is the promise kept? Better question—has the promise been broken? The condition the promise is based on—whether today is your birthday—is not satisfied, so we say that the promise is not broken. The implication is true.

- Today is not your birthday, and I did not bring you a cake. Again, the condition of the promise is not satisfied, so the promise is not broken. The implication is true.

In the last two cases, where the condition of the promise is not satisfied, we sometimes say that the implication is *vacuously true*.

This definition of implication might be a bit counterintuitive to the way we use it in day-to-day speaking. When we say If it rains, then the ground is wet, we usually mean both that If the ground is wet, then it rains and If it rains, then the ground is wet. This is known as biconditional and is denoted as $a \leftrightarrow b$, or simply a iff b.

a	b	$a \rightarrow b$
⊤	⊤	⊤
⊤	⊥	⊥
⊥	⊤	⊤
⊥	⊥	⊤

As stated in Definition 1, propositions can also be defined (or combined) in terms of other propositions. For example, you can choose a to be I like milk and b to be I like sugar. So $a \wedge b$ means that I like both milk and sugar. If you let c be I am cool then with $a \wedge b \to c$, you say: If I like milk and sugar, then I am cool. Note how you can take a proposition $a \wedge b$ and modify it with another connective to form a new proposition.

✎ Exercise 1   Come up with a few propositions and combine them using:

1. The "and" connective

2. The "or" connective

3. The negation connective

4. The implication connective

Try to come up with a sensible statement in English for each derived proposition.

2.1.2. First-order Logic

ⓘ Definition 2   The first-order logical system extends propositional logic by additionally covering **predicates** and **quantifiers**. A predicate $P(x)$ takes an input x, and produces either true or false as output. There are two quantifiers introduced: $\forall$ (universal quantifier) and $\exists$ (existential quantifier).

One example of a predicate is P(x) = x is organic, with $P(Salad) = \top$, but $P(Rock) = \perp$.

In the following example, the universal quantifier says that the predicate will hold for *all* possible choices of x: $\forall x, P(x)$. Alternatively, the existential quantifier says that the predicate will hold for *at least one* choice of x: $\exists x, P(x)$.

Another example of combining a predicate with the universal quantifier is P(x) = x is a mammal, then $\forall x, P(x)$ is true, for all x ranging over the set of humans. You can choose P(x) = x understands Dependent Types with $\exists x, P(x)$ to say that there is at least one person that understands dependent types.

The negation of the quantifiers is defined as follows:

- Negation of universal quantifier: $\neg(\forall x, P(x)) \leftrightarrow \exists x, \neg P(x)$

- Negation of existential quantifier: $\neg(\exists x, P(x)) \leftrightarrow \forall x, \neg P(x)$

As an example, for P(x) = x understands Dependent Types, the negation of $\exists x, P(x)$ is $\forall x, \neg P(x)$. That is, the negation of there is at least one person that understands Dependent Types is for all persons x, x does not understand Dependent Types, or simply put nobody understands Dependent Types.

✎ Exercise 2   Think of a real-world predicate and express its truthiness using the $\forall$ and $\exists$ symbols. Afterward, negate both the universal and existential quantifier.

2.1.3. Higher-order Logic

In first-order logic, predicates act like functions that take an input value and produce a proposition. A predicate can't be true or false until a specific value is substituted for the variables, and the quantifiers ∀ and ∃ "close" over a predicate to give a statement that can be either true or false.

Likewise, we can define a "meta-predicate" that acts as a function on predicates. For example, let $\Gamma(P)$ be the statement there exists a person x such that P(x) is true. Note that it doesn't make sense to ask if $\Gamma(P)$ is true or false until you plug in a specific *predicate P*. But you can quantify over P and construct a statement like $\forall P, \Gamma(P)$. In English, this statement translates to For any given property P, there exists a person satisfying that property.

Meta-predicates like Γ are called *second-order* because they range over first-order predicates. And there's no reason to stop there; you can define third-order predicates that range over second-order predicates, and fourth-order predicates that range over third-order predicates, and so on.

ⓘ Definition 3   The **higher-order logical system** (second-order logic, third-order-logic, ..., higher-order [nth-order] logic) extends the quantifiers that range over individuals[1] to range over predicates.

For example, the second-order logic quantifies over sets. Third-order logic quantifies over sets of sets, and so on.

---

[1] Since unrestricted quantification leads to inconsistency, higher-order logic is an attempt to avoid this. You will look into Russell's paradox later as an example.

Moving up the hierarchy of logical systems brings power, but at a price. Propositional (zeroth-order) logic is completely decidable.[2] Predicate (first-order) logic is no longer decidable, and by Gödel's incompleteness theorem, you have to choose between completeness and consistency, but at least there is still an algorithm that can determine whether a proof is valid or not. For second-order and higher logic, you lose even this—you have to choose between completeness, consistency, and a proof detection algorithm.

The good news is that in practice, second-order predicates are used in a very limited capacity, and third- and higher-order predicates are never needed. One important example of a second-order predicate appears in the Peano axioms of the natural numbers.

ⓘ **Definition 4   Peano axioms** is a system of axioms that describes the natural numbers. It consists of nine axioms, but we name only a few:

1. 0 (zero) is a natural number.

2. For every number x, we have that $S(x)$ is a natural number, namely the successor function.

3. For every number x, we have that $x = x$, namely that equality is reflexive.

---

[2] This means that there is a decidability algorithm—an algorithm that will always return a correct value (e.g., true or false), instead of looping infinitely or producing a wrong answer.

ⓘ Definition 5   The **ninth axiom** in Peano axioms is the induction axiom. It states the following: if P is a predicate where $P(0)$ is true, and for every natural number n, if $P(n)$ is true, then we can prove that $P(n + 1)$ and $P(n)$ is true for all natural numbers.

Peano axioms are expressed using a combination of first-order and second-order logic. This concept consists of a set of axioms for the natural numbers, and all of them are statements in first-order logic. An exception to this is the induction axiom, which is in second-order since it quantifies over predicates. The base axioms can be augmented with arithmetical operations of addition, multiplication, and the order relation, which can also be defined using first-order axioms.

2.2. Set Theory Abstractions

ⓘ Definition 6   Set theory is a type of formal system, which is the most common **foundation of mathematics**. It is a branch of mathematical logic that works with **sets**, which are collections of objects.

Like in programming, building abstractions in mathematics is of equal importance. However, the best way to understand something is to get to the bottom of it. Let's start by working from the lowest level to the top. We start with the most basic object (the unordered collection) and work our way up to defining functions. Functions are an important core concept of Idris; however, as you will see in the theory that Idris relies on, functions are used as a primitive notion (an axiom) instead of being built on top of something else.

ⓘ Definition 7   A set is an **unordered** collection of objects. The objects can be anything.

Finite sets can be denoted by *roster notation*; we write a list of objects in the set, separated by commas, and enclose them using curly braces. For example, one set of fruits is {apple, banana}. Since it is an unordered collection, we have {apple, banana} = {banana, apple}.

ⓘ Definition 8   Set membership states that a given object belongs to a set. It is denoted using the ∈ operator.

For example, apple ∈ {apple, banana} says that apple is in that set.

Roster notation is inconvenient for large sets, and not possible for infinite sets. Another way to define a set is with *set-builder notation*. With this notation, you specify a set by giving a predicate that all of its members satisfy. A typical set in set-builder notation has the form $\{x \mid P(x)\}$, where P is a predicate. If a is a specific object, then $a \in \{x \mid P(x)\}$ precisely when $P(a)$ is true.

ⓘ Definition 9   An *n*-tuple is an **ordered collection** of *n* objects. As with sets, the objects can be anything. Tuples are usually denoted by commas separating the list of objects and enclosing them using parentheses.

For example, you can use the set `{{1, {a1}}, {2, {a2}}, ... , {n, {an}}}` to represent the ordered collection $(a_1, a_2, ..., a_n)$. This will now allow you to extract the k-th element of the tuple, by picking x such that $\{k, \{x\}\} \in A$. Having done that, now you have $(a, b) = (c, d) \equiv a = c \wedge b = d$, that is, two tuples are equal iff their first and second elements respectively are equal. This is what makes them ordered.

One valid tuple is (1 pm, 2 pm, 3 pm) which represents three hours of a day, sequentially.

ⓘ Definition 10   An **_n_-ary relation** is just a set of _n_-tuples.

For example, the `is bigger than` relation represents a 2-tuple (pair), for the following set: `{(cat, mouse), (mouse, cheese), (cat, cheese)}`.

ⓘ Definition 11   _A_ is a subset of _B_ if all elements of _A_ are found in _B_ (but not necessarily vice versa). We denote it as such: $A \subseteq B$.

For example, the expressions $\{1, 2\} \subseteq \{1, 2, 3\}$ and $\{1, 2, 3\} \subseteq \{1, 2, 3\}$ are both true. But this expression is not true: $\{1, 2, 3\} \subseteq \{1, 2\}$.

ⓘ Definition 12   A **Cartesian product** is defined as the set $\{(a, b) \mid a \in A \wedge b \in B\}$. It is denoted as $A \times B$.

For example, if A = `{a, b}` and B = `{1, 2, 3}`, then the combinations are: $A \times B = \{(a, 1), (a, 2), (a, 3), (b, 1), (b, 2), (b, 3)\}$.

> **ⓘ Definition 13   Functions** are defined in terms of relations.[3] A binary (2-tuple) set F represents a mapping[4] from some set A to some set B, where F is a subset of the Cartesian product of A and B. That is, a function f from A to B is denoted $f: A \rightarrow B$ and is a subset of F, that is, $f \subseteq F$. There is one more constraint that functions have, namely, that they cannot produce two or more different values for a single input.

For example, the function $f(x) = x + 1$ is a function that, given a number, returns that number increased by one. We have that $f(1) = 2$, $f(2) = 3$, and so on. Another way to represent this function is using the 2-tuple set: f = {(1, 2), (2, 3), (3, 4), ...}.

One simple way to think of functions is in the form of tables. For a function $f(x)$ accepting a single parameter x, you have a two-column table where the first column is the input and the second column is the output. For a function $f(x, y)$ accepting two parameters x and y, you have a three-column table where the first and second columns represent the input, and

---

[3] It is worth noting that in set theory, P would be a subset of a relation, that is, $P \subseteq A \times \{T, F\}$, where A is a set of some inputs, for example Salad and Rock. When working with other systems, you need to be careful, as this is not the case with first-order logic. In the case of first-order logic, you have $P(Salad) = T$, $P(Rock) = \bot$, and so on. as atomic statements, not mathematical functions (i.e., they cannot be broken down into smaller statements). This is what makes first-order logic independent of set theory. In addition, functions have a nice characterization that is dual to the concepts of "one-to-one" (total) and "onto" (well-defined).

[4] In other words, a function is a subset of all combinations of ordered pairs whose first element is an element of A and the second element is an element of B.

the third column is the output. Thus, the previous function in the form of a table would look like this:

x	f(x)
1	2
2	3
...	...

Exercise 3 Think of a set of objects and express that some object belongs to that set.

Exercise 4 Think of a set of objects whose order matters and express the set in terms of an ordered collection.

Exercise 5 Think of a relation (for example, the relationship between two people in a family tree) and express it using the notation described.

Exercise 6 Come up with two subset expressions—one that is true and one that is false.

Exercise 7 Think of two sets and combine them using the definition of the Cartesian product. Afterward, think of two subset expressions, one that is true and one that is false.

✎ **Exercise 8**   Think of a function and represent it using the table approach.

✎ **Exercise 9**   Write down the corresponding input and output sets for the function you implemented in Exercise 8.

2.3. Substitution and Mathematical Proofs

Substitution lies at the heart of mathematics.[5]

ⓘ**Definition 14   Substitution** consists of systematically replacing occurrences of some symbol with a given value. It can be applied in different contexts involving formal objects containing symbols.

For example, assume that you have the following:

1. An inference rule that states: If $a = b$ and $b = c$, then $a = c$

2. Two axioms that state: $1 = 2$ and $2 = 3$

---

[5] A similar statement can be made about programming, but we cover an interesting case in Appendix C related to **pure** and **impure** functions.

You can use the following "proof" to claim that $1 = 3$:

1. $1 = 2$ (axiom)

2. $2 = 3$ (axiom)

3. $1 = 2$ and $2 = 3$ (from 1 and 2 combined)

4. $1 = 3$, from 3 and the inference rule

In general, $1 = 3$ does not make any sense. But, in the context of the givens, this proof is valid.

ⓘ Definition 15   A **mathematical argument** consists of a list of propositions. Mathematical arguments are used to demonstrate that a claim is true or false.

ⓘ Definition 16   A proof is defined as an inferential **argument** for a list of given mathematical propositions. To prove a mathematical fact, you need to show that the conclusion (the goal that you want to prove) logically follows from the hypothesis (the list of given propositions).

For example, to prove that a goal G follows from a set of given propositions $\{g_1, g_2, \ldots, g_n\}$, you need to show $(g_1 \wedge g_2 \wedge \ldots \wedge g_n) \to G$. Note the relation between the implication connective[6] (conditional statement) and proofs.

---

[6] The turnstile symbol is similar to implication. It is denoted as $\Gamma \vdash A$, where Γ is a set of statements and A is a conclusion. It is $\top$ iff it is impossible for all statements in Γ to be $\top$, and A to be $\bot$. The reason that we have both implication and entailment is that the former is a well-formed formula (that is, the expression belongs to the object language), while the latter is not a well-formed formula. Rather, it's an expression in the meta-language and works on proofs (instead of objects).

✎ **Exercise 10**   With the given axioms of Peano, prove that
$1 = S(0)$ and $2 = S(S(0))$ are natural numbers.

✎ **Exercise 11**   Come up with several axioms and inference rules
and do a proof similar to the previous example.

2.3.1. Proofs by Truth Tables

Here's one claim: The proposition $A \wedge B \to B$ is true for *any* values of
A and B.

❓ How do you convince someone that this proposition is really true?

You can use the one-proof technique, which is to construct a truth
table. To construct a truth table for a given statement, you break the
statement down into atoms and include every subset of the expression.

For example, to prove the statement $A \wedge B \to B$, you can approach it as
follows:

A	B	$A \wedge B$	$A \wedge B \to B$
T	T	T	T
T	⊥	⊥	T
⊥	T	⊥	T
⊥	⊥	⊥	T

> **ⓘ Definition 17**   A mathematical argument is valid iff all of the propositions are true and the conclusion is also true.

Note that wherever $A \wedge B$ is true (the list of given propositions, or premises, or hypothesis), then so is $A \wedge B \rightarrow B$ (the conclusion), which means that this is a valid logical argument according to Definition 17.

At the lowest level (formal systems), proofs were just a transformation (substitution) from one expression to another. However, at a higher level (logic), the way proofs are done is closely related to the symbols defined in the system. For example, in logic, there's $\wedge$ so there are specific rules about introducing/eliminating it.

✎ Exercise 12   Given the two propositions $A \vee B$ and $\neg B$, prove (or conclude) A by means of a truth table.

Hint: The statement to prove is $((A \vee B) \wedge \neg B) \rightarrow A$.

2.3.2. Three-column Proofs

As previously defined, an argument is a list of statements. There are several ways to do mathematical proofs. One of them is by using the so-called three-column proofs. For this technique, you construct a table with three columns: number of steps, step (or expression derived), and reasoning (explanation of how you got to the particular step).

ⓘ Definition 18   Modus ponens (method of affirming) and **modus tollens** (method of denying) are two inference rules in logic. Their definitions are as follows:

1. Modus ponens states: If you are given $p \rightarrow q$ and p, then you can conclude q.

2. Modus tollens states: If you are given $p \rightarrow q$ and $\neg q$, then you can conclude $\neg p$.

For example, given $A \vee B$, $B \rightarrow C$, $\neg C$, prove A. You can approach the proof as follows:

No.	Step	Reasoning
1	$A \vee B$	Given
2	$B \rightarrow C$	Given
3	$\neg C$	Given
4	$(B \rightarrow C) \wedge \neg C$	2 and 3
5	$\neg B$	Modus tollens rule on 4, i.e. $(p \rightarrow q \wedge \neg q) \rightarrow \neg p$
6	$(A \vee B) \wedge \neg B$	1 and 5
7	A	6, where $p \wedge \neg p$ is a contradiction, i.e. invalid argument

? Proofs with truth tables look a lot easier than column proofs. You just plug in the truth values and simplify, where column proofs require planning ahead. Why would you bother with column proofs?

Proofs with truth tables work for only propositional (zeroth order) theorems—the table method is essentially the decidability algorithm for zeroth-order logic. That's why they are easy (if verbose) and always work, and why column proofs become necessary once you're using quantifiers.

✎ Exercise 13   Prove $((A \vee B) \wedge \neg B) \to A$ using the three-column proof technique.

2.3.3. Formal Proofs

You've seen how to construct proofs with truth tables. However, if your statements involve the use of quantifiers, then doing proofs with truth tables is impossible. Three-column proofs, in contrast, contain many details. Ideally, the proof should be short, clear, and concise about what you want to prove. Therefore, let's try to prove a statement by means of a formal proof.

To prove $A \wedge B \to B$, you start by assuming that $A \wedge B$ is true since otherwise, the statement is vacuously true by definition for implication. If $A \wedge B$ is true, then both A and B are true by definition of and, that is, you can conclude B.

Do not worry if the previous paragraph sounded too magical. There is not much magic involved. Usually, it comes down to using a few rules (or "tricks", if you will) for how you can use given information and achieve your goal. These proof techniques are summarized in the following table:

Goal Form	Technique to Prove It
$P \rightarrow Q$	Assume that P is true and prove Q.
$\neg P$	Assume that P is true and arrive at a contradiction.
$P1 \wedge P2 \wedge \ldots \wedge Pn$	Prove each one of $P1, P2, \ldots, Pn$ separately.
$P1 \vee P2 \vee \ldots \vee Pn$	Prove that at least one of $P1, P2, \ldots, Pn$.
$P \leftrightarrow Q$	Prove both $P \rightarrow Q$ and $Q \rightarrow P$.
$\forall x, P(x)$	Assume that x is an arbitrary object and prove that $P(x)$.
$\exists x, P(x)$	Find an x such that $P(x)$ is true.
$\exists! x, P(x)$[7]	Prove $\exists x, P(x)$ (existence) and $\forall x \forall y, (P(x) \wedge P(y) \rightarrow x = y)$ (uniqueness) separately.

Given Form	Technique to Use It
$P \rightarrow Q$	If P is also given, then conclude that Q (by modus ponens).
$\neg P$	If P can be proven true, then conclude a contradiction.
$P1 \wedge P2 \wedge \ldots \wedge Pn$	Treat each one of $P1, P2, \ldots, Pn$ as a given.
$P1 \vee P2 \vee \ldots \vee Pn$	Use proof by cases, where in each case you assume one of $P1, P2, \ldots, Pn$.
$P \leftrightarrow Q$	Conclude both $P \rightarrow Q$ and $Q \rightarrow P$.
$\forall x, P(x)$	For any x, conclude that $P(x)$.
$\exists x, P(x)$	Introduce a new variable, say $x0$, so that $P(x0)$ is true.
$\exists! x, P(x)$	Introduce a new variable, say $x1$, so that $P(x1)$ is true. You can also use $\forall x \forall y, (P(x) \wedge P(y) \rightarrow x = y)$.

---

[7] The notation $\exists!$ stands for *unique existential quantifier*. It means that *only one* object fulfills the predicate, as opposed to $\exists$, which states that at least one object fulfills the predicate.

For example, you can use these techniques to perform the following proofs:

1. $A \land B \to A \lor B$. To prove this goal, assume $A \land B$ and use proof by cases:

    1. Proof for A: Since you're given $A \land B$, you are also given A. Thus, A

    2. Proof for B: Since you're given $A \land B$, you are also given B. Thus, B

    3. Thus, $A \lor B$

2. $A \land B \leftrightarrow B \land A$. To prove this goal, you need to prove both sides for the implications:

    1. Proof for $A \land B \to B \land A$: You can assume that $A \land B$, thus you have both A and B. To prove the goal of $B \land A$, you need to prove B and A separately, which you already have as given.

    2. Proof for $B \land A \to A \land B$. You can assume that $B \land A$, thus you have both B and A. To prove the goal of $A \land B$, you need to prove A and B separately, which you already have as given.

    3. Thus, $A \land B \leftrightarrow B \land A$.

3. $\forall x, x = x$. You know that for any number x, this number is equal to itself. Thus, $\forall x, x = x$.

4. $\exists x, x > 0$. To prove this, you only need to find an x that is greater than 1. One valid example is 1. Thus, $\exists x, x > 0$.

🖉 **Exercise 14**   Prove $((A \lor B) \land \neg B) \to A$ by means of a formal proof.

🖉 **Exercise 15**   We've used the rules modus tollens and modus ponens without giving an actual proof for them. Try to prove by yourself that these two rules hold, by constructing a truth table and by using a three-column proof:

1.   Modus tollens: $((p \to q) \land \neg q) \to \neg p$
2.   Modus ponens: $((p \to q) \land p) \to q$

🖉 **Exercise 16**   Prove the formal proofs 1 and 2 from the previous examples using both truth tables and three-column proofs techniques.

🖉 **Exercise 17**   Think of a proposition and try to prove it by means of a formal proof.

2.3.4. Mathematical Induction

ⓘ **Definition 19   Recursive functions** are functions that refer to themselves. We have the following properties for such functions:

1. A simple base case (or cases) is a terminating case that returns a value without using recursion.

2. A set of rules that reduce the other cases toward the base case.

ⓘ **Definition 20   Mathematical induction** is a proof method that is used to prove that a predicate $P(n)$ is true for all natural numbers, n. It consists of proving two parts: a base case and an inductive step.

1. For the **base case**, you need to show that what you want to prove $P(n)$ is true for some starting value k, which is usually 0.

2. For the **inductive step**, you need to prove that $P(n) \rightarrow P(n + 1)$, that is, if you assume that $P(n)$ is true, then $P(n + 1)$ must follow as a consequence.

After proving the two parts, you can conclude that $P(n)$ holds for all natural numbers. The formula that you need to prove is $P(0) \wedge (P(n) \rightarrow P(n + 1))$.

To understand why mathematical induction works, it is best to visualize dominoes arranged in a sequence. If you push over the first domino, it will push over the second, which will push over the third, and so on. That is, if you position the dominoes such that if one falls, it will push over the next one, that is, $P(n)$ implies $P(n + 1)$, and you push the first one $P(0)$, then all the dominoes will fall, so $P(n)$ is true in general.

ⓘ Definition 21   We are given this recursive definition for adding numbers:

1. Zero is a left identity for addition, that is $n = 0 + n$.

2. $S(m) + n = S(m + n)$, where S is the successor function, that is $S(0) = 1$, $S(1) = 2$, and so on.

For example, in order to prove that $\forall n, n + 0 = n$ in the system of Peano axioms, you can proceed by induction (which is an axiom in this system). For the base case, you have $0 + 0 = 0$, which is true (by definition of adding numbers, for $n = 0$). For the inductive step, you first assume that $n+0 = n$ is true and prove that $S(n)+0 = S(n)$. By definition of addition, you have $S(n) + 0 = S(n + 0)$. If you use the inductive hypothesis, you have $S(n + 0) = S(n)$, which is what you needed to show.

CHAPTER 3

Type Theory

Some type theories can serve as an alternative foundation of mathematics, as opposed to standard set theory. One such well-known type theory is Martin-Löf's intuitionistic theory of types, which is an extension of Alonzo Church's simply-typed λ-calculus. Before you begin working with Idris, you will become familiar with the theories upon which Idris is built as a language.

ⓘDefinition 1   Type theory is defined as a class of formal systems. In these theories, every object is joined with a type, and operations upon these objects are constrained by the joined types. To say that x is of type X, we denote $x : X$. Functions are a primitive concept in type theory.[1]

---

[1] Unlike in set theory, where they are defined in terms of relations.

© Boro Sitnikovski 2023
B. Sitnikovski, *Introduction to Dependent Types with Idris*,
https://doi.org/10.1007/978-1-4842-9259-4_3

For example, with 1 : Nat, 2 : Nat, you can say that 1 and 2 are of type Nat, that is natural numbers. An operation (function) + : Nat → Nat → Nat is interpreted as a function that takes two objects of type Nat and returns an object of type Nat.

ⓘ **Definition 2**   In type theory, a **type constructor** is a function that builds new types from old ones. This function accepts types as parameters and returns a new type.

Idris supports algebraic data types. These data types are a kind of complex types, that is, types constructed by combining other types. Two classes of algebraic types are **product types** and **sum types**.

ⓘ **Definition 3**   **Algebraic data types** are types where you can additionally specify the form for each of the elements. They are called "algebraic" in the sense that the types are constructed using algebraic operations. The algebra here is sum and product:

1. Sum (union) is an alternation. It is denoted as A | B and it means that a constructed value is either of type A or B.

2. Product is a combination. It is denoted as A B and it means that a constructed value is a pair where the first element is of type A, and the second element is of type B.

To understand the algebra they capture, you denote with $|A|$ the number of possible values of type A. When you create an algebraic sum, you have $|A \mid B| = |A| + |B|$. Similarly, for an algebraic product, you have $|A\ B| = |A| * |B|$.

As an example, assume that you have two types: Nat for natural numbers, and Real for real numbers. Using sum (union), you can construct a new type Nat | Real. Valid values of this type are 1 : Nat | Real, 3.14 : Nat | Real, and so on. Using product, you can construct a new type called Nat Real. Valid values of this type are 1 1.5 : Nat Real, 2 3.14 : Nat Real, and so on. Using this approach, sums and products can be combined and thus more complex data structures can be defined.

The Bool type has two possible values: True and False. Thus, |Bool| = 2. The type Unit (equivalent to ()) has one possible value: Unit. You can now form a sum type Bool | Unit, which has length 3 and values True, False, and Unit. Additionally, the product type Bool Unit has length 2 and values True Unit and False Unit.

Besides the sum and product, there is another important operation called *exponentiation*. This corresponds to functions, so a type $a \to b$ has $|b|^{|a|}$ possible values. Section 3.3 explains how this algebra can be generalized.

Finally, Idris supports dependent types.[2] These kinds of types are so powerful that they can encode most properties of programs. With their help, Idris can prove invariants at compile time. As you will see in Section 4.2,

---

[2] Dependent types allow proofs of statements involving first-order predicates, compared to simple types that correspond to propositional logic. While useful (since you can check whether an expression fulfills a given condition at compile-time), dependent types add complexity to a type system. In order to calculate type "equality" of dependent types, computations are necessary. If you allow any values for dependent types, then solving equality of a type may involve deciding whether two programs produce the same result. Thus, the check may become undecidable.

types also allow you to encode mathematical proofs, which brings computer programs closer to mathematical proofs. As a consequence, this allows you to prove properties (e.g., specifications) about your software.[3]

❓Why are types useful?   Russell's paradox (per the mathematician Bertrand Russell) states the following: In a village in which there is only one barber, there is a rule whereby the barber shaves anyone who doesn't shave themself, and no one else. So, who shaves the barber? Suppose the barber shaves himself. Then, he's one of those who shaves themselves, but the barber shaves only those who do not shave themselves, which is a contradiction. Alternatively, if you assume that the barber does not shave himself, then he is in the group of people whom the barber shaves, which again is a contradiction. Apparently then the barber does not shave himself, but he also doesn't *not* shave himself—a paradox.

Some set theories are affected by Russell's paradox. As a response to this, between 1902 and 1908, Bertrand Russell himself proposed different type theories as an attempt to resolve the issue. By joining types to values, you can avoid the paradox because, in this theory, every set is defined as having elements from a distinct type, for example, Type 1. Elements from Type 1 can be included in a different set, say, elements of Type 2, and so forth. Thus, the paradox is no longer an issue since the set of elements of Type 1 cannot be

---

[3] This is what makes Idris a so-called proof assistant. In general, Idris combines a lot of functionalities from mainstream languages (Java, C, and C++) and some functionalities from proof assistants, which further blurs the line between these two kinds of software.

contained in their own set, since the types do not match. In a way, we're adding hierarchy to sets in order to resolve the issue of "self-referential" sets. This is also the case with Idris, where we have that Type : Type 1 : Type 2, and so on.

Thus, for Russell's paradox specifically, if you set the type of a person to be P, then the list of people would be of type List P. However, there is no way to express {P} such that P ∈ P, since List P only contains elements of type P, and not List P.

3.1. Lambda Calculus

Lambda calculus is a formal system for expressing computation.[4] The grammar rules are divided in two parts: function abstraction and function application. Function abstraction defines what a function does, and function application "computes" a function. For example, $f(x) = x + 1$ is a function abstraction and $f(3)$ is a function application. The equality sign = is replaced with a dot, and instead of writing $f(x)$, you write λx. To represent $f(x) = x + 1$, you write $\lambda x.x + 1$. Parentheses allow you to specify the order of evaluation.

---

[4] A *Turing machine* is a very simple abstract machine designed to capture our intuitive understanding of *computation* in the most general sense. Any formal system that can simulate a Turing machine, and thus also perform arbitrary computations, is called *Turing complete*.

ⓘ Definition 4   The set of symbols for the lambda calculus is defined as:

1. There are variables v1, v2, ...

2. There are only two abstract symbols: . and λ

3. There are parentheses: (and)

The set of grammar rules Λ for well-formed expressions is defined as:

1. If x is a variable, then x ∈ Λ

2. If x is a variable and M ∈ Λ, then (λx.M) ∈ Λ (rule of abstraction)

3. If M, N ∈ Λ, then (M N) ∈ Λ (rule of application)

Some examples of well-formed expressions are λf x.f x and λf x.f(f x). In fact, you can encode numbers this way. The first expression can be thought of as the number 1, and the second as the number 2. In other words, the number 1 is defined roughly as f(x), and 2 as f (f(x)). Note that f and x do not have special definitions; they are abstract objects. This encoding is known as the *Church encoding*. Operations on numbers (plus, minus, and so on) and other data such as Booleans and lists can also be encoded similarly.

Note that λf x.f x is shorthand for λf.λx.f x.

✏ **Exercise 1**   Convince yourself that the expression $\lambda f\ x.f\ x$ is a well-formed expression by writing down each one of the grammar rules used.

3.1.1. Term Reduction

Every variable in a lambda expression can be characterized as either free or bound in that expression.

ℹ **Definition 5**   A variable in a lambda expression is called **free** if it does not appear inside at least one lambda body where it is found in the abstraction. Alternatively, if it does appear inside at least one lambda body, then the variable is bound at the innermost such lambda abstraction.

This definition of "bound" corresponds roughly to the concept of scope in many programming languages. Lambda expressions introduce a new scope in which their argument variables are bound.

For example, in the expression $\lambda y.x\ y$, we have that y is a bound variable, and x is a free one. Variable binding in lambda calculus is subtle but important, so let's see some trickier examples:

- In $x(\lambda x.x)$, the leftmost x is free, while the rightmost x is bound by the lambda.

- In $(\lambda x.x)(\lambda x.x)$, both occurrences of x are bound; the first at the left lambda, and the second at the right lambda.

- In $\lambda x.(\lambda x.x)$, the sole occurrence of x is certainly bound. Now there are two potential "binding sites"— the inner lambda and the outer lambda. Given a choice like this, you should always say the variable is bound at the innermost lambda.

The distinction between free and bound variables becomes important when you ask whether two different lambda expressions are "equal." For instance, consider the two expressions $\lambda x.x$ and $\lambda y.y$. Syntactically these are not the same; they use different characters for the variable. But semantically they are identical, because in lambda calculus, variables bound by a lambda are "dummy" variables whose exact names are not important. When two lambda expressions differ only by a consistent renaming of the bound variables like this, we say they are *alpha equivalent*.

There are two other useful notions of semantic equivalence for lambda expressions: beta and eta equivalence.

ⓘ **Definition 6**   The rules of **terms reduction** (inference rules) allow you to compute (simplify) lambda expressions. There are three types of reduction:

1. α - (alpha) reduction: Renaming bound variables

2. β - (beta) reduction: Applying arguments to functions

3. η - (eta) reduction: Two functions are "equal" iff they return the same result for all arguments

---

For example, for the expression $(\lambda x.f\ x)\ y$, you can use alpha reduction to get to $(\lambda z.f\ z)\ y$, by changing x to z. Using beta reduction, the expression can further be reduced to just $f\ y$, since you "consumed" the z by removing it from the abstraction and wherever it occurred in the body you just replaced it with what was applied to it, that is y. Finally, with eta reduction, you can rewrite (λx.f x) to just f, since they are equivalent.

Given these rules, you can define the successor function as SUCC = λn f x .f(n f x). Now try to apply 1 to SUCC:

1. Evaluating SUCC 1 =

2. Substitute the n definitions of SUCC and 1: (λn f x.f(n f x)) (λf x.f x) =

3. Apply 1 to SUCC (i.e., "consume" n by beta reduction): λf x.f((λf x.f x) f x) =

4. Finally, apply f and x to a function that accepts f and x (which is just the body of the abstraction): λf x.f(f x) = 2

ⓘ Definition 7   A **fixed-point combinator** is any function that satisfies the equation fix f = f(fix f).

One example of such a combinator is Y = λf.(λx.f(x x)) (λx.f (x x)). This definition satisfies Y f = f(Y f). This combinator allows for recursion in lambda calculus. Since it is impossible to refer to the function within its body, recursion can only be achieved by applying parameters to a function, which is what this combinator does.

✎ Exercise 2   Evaluate SUCC 2 to determine the definition of number 3.

✐ **Exercise 3**   Come up with your own functions that operate on the Church numerals. It can be as simple as returning the same number or a constant one.

3.2. Lambda Calculus with Types

So far this chapter has discussed the *untyped* lambda calculus, but it is possible to augment the rules of lambda calculus so that variables are *typed*. This makes it possible to add a statically checked layer of semantics to a lambda expression so you can ensure that values are used in a consistent and meaningful way. There are several ways to add types to lambda calculus, and the goal is to approach the full *dependent* type system of Idris. As a stepping stone, let's first consider *simple* types.

ⓘ **Definition 8**   Simply typed lambda calculus is a type theory that adds types to lambda calculus. It joins the system with a unique type constructor → which constructs types for functions. The formal definition and the set of lambda expressions are similar to that of lambda calculus, with the addition of types.

The set of symbols for this system is defined as follows:

1. There are variables v1, v2, ...

2. There are only two abstract symbols: . and λ

3. There are parentheses: (and)

The set of grammar rules Λ for well-formed expressions is defined as:

1. If x is a variable, then $x \in \Lambda$.

2. If x is a variable and $M \in \Lambda$, then $(\lambda x.M) \in \Lambda$ (rule of abstraction).

3. If $M, N \in \Lambda$, then $(M\ N) \in \Lambda$ (rule of application).

4. If x is a variable, T is a type, and $M \in \Lambda$, then $(\lambda x : T.M) \in \Lambda$.

5. If x is a variable and T is a type, then $x : T \in \Lambda$.

There is a single type constructor:

1. For some type A, the type constructor T is defined as
   $A \mid T \rightarrow T$.

That is, an expression in this system can additionally be an abstraction with x having joined a type (rule 4) or an expression of a variable having joined a type T (rule 5), where the type constructor is a sum type and it says that you either have primitive types or a way to form new types. In an attempt to redefine Church numerals and the successor function, you have to be careful, as the types of these definitions have to match. Let's recall the Church numerals:

1. Number 1, that is, $\lambda f\ x.f\ x$

2. Number 2, that is, $\lambda f\ x.f(f\ x)$

Given the definition of 1, its type must have the form $(a \rightarrow b) \rightarrow a \rightarrow b$ for some values a and b. You are expecting to be able to apply f to x, and so if $x : a$ then $f : a \rightarrow b$ in order for the types to match correctly. With similar reasoning, you have the same type for 2. At this point, you have the type of $(a \rightarrow b) \rightarrow a \rightarrow b$. Finally, with the given definition of 2, note that expressions of type b need to be able to be passed to functions of type $a \rightarrow b$, since the result of applying f to x serves as the argument of f. The most general way for that to be true is if a = b. As a result, you have the type $(a \rightarrow a) \rightarrow a \rightarrow a$. You can denote this type definition to be Nat. These are the numbers:

1. Number 1 becomes $\lambda[f : (a \rightarrow a)]$ $[x : a].f\ x : Nat$

2. Number 2 becomes $\lambda[f : (a \rightarrow a)]$ $[x : a].f (f\ x) : Nat$

The (typed) successor function is SUCC = $\lambda[n : Nat]$ $[f : (a \rightarrow a)]$ $[x : a].f(n\ f\ x) : Nat \rightarrow Nat$.

Simply typed lambda calculus sits in a sweet spot on the spectrum of type systems. It is powerful enough to do useful work, but also simple enough to have strong properties. Simple types have limitations when compared to full dependent types, discussed in the next section, but their great trade-off is the existence of a full *inference algorithm*. The strategy used to determine the type of a lambda expression from the bottom up is the core of the widely used Hindley-Damas-Milner algorithm for type inference, which can automatically *infer* the simple type of a lambda expression without requiring any explicit type annotations from the programmer.

Fixed-point combinators do not exist in the simply-typed lambda calculus.[5] To see why, consider the function fix = $\lambda[f : a \rightarrow a] : a$. You can apply fix to some element $x : a \rightarrow a$. Thus, fix $x : a$, but x = fix x is a type error because the infinite type $a \rightarrow a$ = a cannot be matched.

---

[5] For this reason, the typed lambda calculus is not Turing complete, while the untyped lambda calculus is. Fixed-point combinators provide flexibility, but that has its drawbacks. They can be non-terminating and loop indefinitely without producing an answer. While non-termination has its uses for software (e.g., a program keeps running until you choose to close it), termination is important for mathematical proofs, as you will see in Section 4.2.

Exercise 4   Come up with a definition of the typed number 3.

 Exercise 5   Apply the typed 1 to SUCC and confirm that the result is 2. Make sure you confirm that the types also match in the process of evaluation.

 Exercise 6   In Exercise 3, you were asked to come up with a function. Try to figure out the type of this function or, if not applicable, come up with a new function and then figure out its type using the previous reasoning.

3.3. Dependent Types

In the simply-typed lambda calculus, *values* and *types* are fundamentally different kinds of things that are related only by the "has type" predicate, :. Values are allowed to depend on values—these are lambda abstractions. And types are allowed to depend on types—these are arrow types. But types are not allowed to depend on values. A *dependent typing* system lifts this restriction.

Definition 9   **Dependent types** are types that depend on values.

A list of numbers is a type (List Nat, for example). However, a list of numbers whose length is bounded by some constant, or whose entries are increasing, is a dependent type.

ⓘ **Definition 10**   A **dependent product type** is a collection of types B : A → U where for each element a : A, there's an assigned type B(a) : U, where U is a universe of types.[6] We say that B(a) varies with a. It is denoted as $\prod(x : A)$, B(x) or $\prod\limits_{x:A} B(x)$.

This definition might seem a bit scary and tricky to grasp, but it really is simple, and it is best to see it in action through the following example:

1. The universe of types contains all possible types. For example, Type, Nat, and so on, so U = {Type, Nat, List n, ...}.

2. The collection of types of interest is List n, which represents a list of n elements. That is, A = {List n}.

The definition states that in the universe U, there exists a function B(n) = List n. B is the collection of functions that, given a number n, will return a list of n numbers. For example, say you have the following lists:

1. List of one element: [1] : B(1), that is [1] : List 1

2. List of two elements: [1, 2] : List 2

3. List of n elements: [1, 2, ... , n] : List n

---

[6] Collections, in general, are considered to be subcollections of some large universal collection, also called the *universe*. Depending on the context, the definition of this universe will vary.

In general, you have a function that takes an n and produces a List n, that is, f : $\prod$(x : Nat), n → List n or simply f : n → List n, where the possible types for it are f : 1 → List 1, f : 2 → List 2, and so on. You've just constructed your first dependent type!

ℹ **Definition 11   A dependent sum type** can be used to represent indexed pairs, where the type of the second element depends on the type of the first element. That is, if you have a : A and b : B(a), this makes a sum type. Denote it as Σ(x : A), B(x) or $\sum\limits_{x:A} B(x)$.

For example, if you set A = Nat, and B(a) = List a, then you form the dependent sum type Σ(x : Nat), List x. Possible types for it are (1, List 1) or (2, List 2), and so on. For example, you can construct the following pairs: (1, [1]), (2, [1, 2]), (3, [1, 2, 3]), and so on.

Dependent types generalize product and exponentiation. Namely, Σ (multiplication) is a generalization of the product type where the type of the second element depends on the first element, and $\prod$ (exponentiation) is a generalization of the exponentiation type where the resulting type of a function depends on its input.

✏ **Exercise 7**   Think of a way to construct a different dependent product type and express it by using the previous reasoning.

✏ **Exercise 8**   Think of a way to construct a different dependent sum type and express it using the previous reasoning.

3.4. Intuitionistic Theory of Types

The core "construct" in Idris are types. As you've seen, foundations are based on type theory. In classical mathematical logic, you have sets and propositions, according to set theory.

The intuitionistic theory of types (or constructive type theory) offers an alternative foundation to mathematics. This theory was introduced by Martin-Löf, a Swedish mathematician, in 1972. It is based on the isomorphism (or "equality") that propositions are types.

Proving a theorem in this system consists of constructing[7] (or providing evidence for) a particular object. If you want to prove something about a type A and you know that a : A, then a is one proof for A. Note how we say *one* proof, because there can be many other elements of type A.

Propositions can also be defined through types. For example, in order to prove that 4 = 4, you need to find an object x of type 4 = 4 (that is x : 4 = 4). One such object is refl (which can be thought of as an axiom), which stands for reflexivity. It states that x = x for all x.

One point worth noting is that in Idris there are "two" types of truths: Bool and Type. Even though there is some similarity (in terms of proofs), in Idris they are fundamentally different. The Bool type can have a value of True or False, while the Type type is either provable or not provable.[8]

---

[7] Because you need to construct an object as evidence in order to prove something, the law of excluded middle P ∨ ¬P is not valid in this logic, whereas in classical mathematical logic this is taken as an axiom. For some propositions, for example, P is an odd number or not, there are proofs that you can provide. However, for some propositions this is impossible, for example, P is a program that halts or not. Unlike classical mathematical logic, in this logic, the law of excluded middle does not exist due to the undecidability problem.

[8] It is provable when you can construct an object of such a type, and not provable otherwise.

This system is useful since, with the use of computer algorithms, you can find a constructive proof for some object (assuming it exists). As a consequence, this is why it can be considered a way to make a programming language act like a proof assistant.

ⓘ Definition 12   The set of grammar rules $\wedge$ for well-formed expressions is defined as follows:

1. s : Type $\in \wedge$ means that s is a well-formed type.

2. $t : s \in \wedge$ means that t is a well-formed expression of type s.

3. $s = t \in \wedge$ means that s and t are the same type.

4. $t = u : s \in \wedge$ means that t and u are equal expressions of type s.

The type constructors are as follows:

1. $\prod$ types and Σ types, as discussed earlier

2. Finite types, for example the nullary (empty) type 0 or $\perp$, the unary type 1 or $\top$, and the Boolean type 2

3. The equality type, where for given a, b : A, the expression a = b represents proof of equality. There is a canonical element a = a, that is, an "axiom" for the reflexivity proof: $\texttt{refl}$: $\prod(a : A)$ a = a Inductive (or recursive) types.

4. This way, you can implement a special form of recursion—one that always terminates, and you will see the importance of this with total functions. Additionally, you can implement product and sum types, which encode conjunction and disjunction respectively.

The inference rules are as follows:

1. The rule of type equality states that if an object is of a type A, and there is another type B equal to A, then that object is of type B: $(a : A, A = B) \rightarrow (a : B)$.

There are also other inference rules, for example introduction and elimination. Section 4.2 shows an example of using these rules.

As an example, for well-formed expressions, rule 1 says that you can form an expression such that an object inhabits the Type type, so an example of a well-formed expression is 1 : Nat, per rule 2, and Nat : Type per rule 1.

A valid type as per the fourth rule of type constructors is the definition of natural numbers Nat = Z | S Nat. Some valid values are Z : Nat, S Z : Nat, and so on.

Exercise 9   We used rule 1 and rule 2 in the example earlier. Try to come up with different ways to use some of the rules.

Exercise 10   Combine the use of rules along with the connectives described earlier to come up with a recursive type and then construct some new objects from it.

3.4.1. Intuitionistic Logic

ⓘ **Definition 13**   A **constructive proof** proves the existence of a mathematical object by creating or constructing the object itself. This is contrary to non-constructive proofs, which prove the existence of objects without giving a concrete example.

ⓘ **Definition 14**   **Intuitionistic logic**, also known as constructive logic, is a type of logic that is different than classical logic in that it "works" with the notion of constructive proof.

ⓘ **Definition 15**   The **BHK (Brouwer-Heyting-Kolmogorov) interpretation** is a mapping of intuitionistic logic to classical mathematical logic, namely:

1. A proof of $P \wedge Q$ is a product type A B, where a is a proof of (or, object of type) P and b is a proof of Q.

2. A proof of $P \vee Q$ is a product type A B, where a is 0 and b is a proof of P, or a is 1 and b is a proof of Q.

3. A proof of $P \rightarrow Q$ is a function f that converts a proof of P to a proof of Q.

4. A proof of $\exists x \in S : f(x)$ is a pair A B, where a is an element of S and b is a proof of $f(a)$ (dependent sum types).

5. A proof of $\forall x \in S \,:\, f(x)$ is a function f that converts an element a from S to a proof of $f(a)$ (dependent product types).

6. A proof of ¬P is defined as $P \rightarrow \perp$, that is, the proof is a function f that converts a proof of P to a proof of $\perp$.

7. There is no proof of $\perp$.

For example, to prove distributivity of $\wedge$ with respect to $\vee$, that is, $P \wedge (Q \vee R) = (P \wedge Q) \vee (P \wedge R)$, you need to construct a proof for the function of type $f \,:\, P(Q \mid R) \rightarrow P \; Q \mid P \; R$. That is, a function that takes a product type of P and sum type of Q and R and returns a sum type of product P and Q and product P and R. Here's the function that accomplishes that:

```
1  f (x, left y) = left (x, y)
2  f (x, right y') = right (x, y')
```

This notation (which is pretty similar to how you write it in Idris) uses (x, y) to denote product type, that is, extract values from a product-type pair, and left and right to denote value constructors for sum type in order to extract values from a sum-type pair. The next chapter introduces Idris and its syntax.

✎ **Exercise 11**   Try to use some of the proofs in the earlier chapters as motivation and work them out by using intuitionistic logic.

CHAPTER 4

Programming in Idris

This chapter introduces the Idris syntax and then defines its functions and types.

Depending on the level of abstraction you are working on, types and proofs can give you a kind of security based on some truths you take for granted (axioms). In fact, this is how you develop code on a daily basis, as a software engineer. You have a list of axioms, for example, a foreach loop in a programming language, and build abstractions from it, expecting the foreach to behave in a certain way. However, this security is not always easy to achieve. For example, consider a scenario where you have a button that is supposed to download a PDF document. In order to prove that it works as expected, you must first pick the abstraction level you will be working on, and then proceed by defining software requirements (what is a PDF, what is a download). So, you first have to define your **specifications**, and then you can proceed with proving correctness.

Even though it's a research language, Idris still has its own uses. It is a Turing complete language, which means that it has the same expressive power as other programming languages, such as Java and C++.

To start, download Idris via www.idris-lang.org/download and install it.

© Boro Sitnikovski 2023
B. Sitnikovski, *Introduction to Dependent Types with Idris*,
https://doi.org/10.1007/978-1-4842-9259-4_4

4.1. Basic Syntax and Definitions

There are two working modes in Idris: REPL (read-evaluate-print-loop), which is interactive mode, and compilation of code. This chapter works mostly in the interactive mode.

You can copy any of the example codes to a file, say test.idr, and launch Idris in REPL mode by writing idris test.idr. This will allow you to interact with Idris given the definitions in the file. If you change the contents of the file, that is, update the definitions, you can use the :r command while in REPL mode to reload the definitions.

4.1.1. Defining Functions

Let's begin by defining a simple function:

```
1  add_1 : Nat -> Nat
2  add_1 x = x + 1
```

With this code, you 're defining a function $f(x) = x+1$, where x is natural number and $f(x)$ (the result) is also a natural number.[1] The first line—add_1 : Nat -> Nat—is called a *type signature*, and it specifies the type of the function; in this case, it's a function that takes a natural number and returns a natural number. The second line—add_1 x = x + 1—is the definition of the function, which states that if add_1 is called with a number x, the result will be x + 1. As you can see in the example, every function has to be provided a type definition. You can interact as follows in the REPL mode:

---

[1] It is worth noting that Haskell has types and kinds. Kinds are similar to types, that is, they are defined as one level above types in simply-typed lambda calculus. For example, types such as Nat have a kind Nat :: * and it's stated that Nat is of kind *. Types such as Nat -> Nat have a kind of * -> *. Since in Idris the types are first-class citizens, there is no distinction between types and kinds.

```
1  Idris> add_1 5
2  6 : Nat
```

Idris shows the result as 6, which is of type Nat. Constants are defined similarly; you can think of them as functions with no arguments.

```
1  number_1 : Nat
2  number_1 = 1
```

As in Haskell, you can use pattern matching. What happens during this phase is that Idris does a check (match) against the definitions of the function and uses the definition of the function that matches the value.

```
1  is_it_zero : Nat -> Bool
2  is_it_zero Z = True
3  is_it_zero x = False
```

You've just defined a function that accepts a natural number and returns a Boolean value (True or False). The first line specifies its type. The second line pattern-matches against the input Z and returns True in that case. The third line pattern-matches against the input x (which is all remaining inputs except Z). In this case, it returns False. Depending on the input, this code will branch the computation to the corresponding definition. Note that Z corresponds to 0 for the type Nat.

Exercise 1   Write a function called my_identity that accepts a natural number and returns the same number.

Exercise 2   Write a function called five_if_zero that accepts a natural number and returns 5 when called with an argument of 0 or otherwise returns the same number. For example, five_if_zero 0 should return 5. five_if_zero 123 should return 123.

4.1.2. Defining and Inferring Types

In Idris, types are first-class citizens. This means that types can be computed and passed to other functions. You define new types by using the keyword data. All concrete types (like Nat) and type constructors (like List) begin with an uppercase letter, while lowercase letters are reserved for polymorphic types.[2] There are a couple of ways to define types. One example is by using the so-called Haskell98 syntax:

```
1  data A a b = A_inst a b
```

This will create a polymorphic type that accepts two type arguments, a and b. Valid constructed types are A Nat Bool, A Nat Nat, and so on. A is a type constructor (a function that returns a type) and A_inst[3] is a value constructor (a function that returns a value of type A a b).

```
1  Idris> A_inst True True
2  A_inst True True : A Bool Bool
3  Idris> A_inst Z True
4  A_inst 0 True : A Nat Bool
```

Note how the type changes depending on what values you pass to the constructor, due to polymorphism.

Here's an equivalent definition by using the GADT (Generalized Algebraic Data Types) syntax:

```
1  data A : Type -> Type -> Type where
2      A_inst : a -> b -> A a b
```

---

[2] A polymorphic type can accept additional types as arguments, which are either defined by the programmer or primitive ones.

[3] The value and type constructors must be named differently since types and values are at the same level in Idris.

This is equivalent to the following definition, which defines an empty data structure along with an axiom for the value constructor:

```
1  data A : Type -> Type -> Type
2  postulate A_inst : a -> b -> A a b
```

With the postulate keyword, you can define axioms that are functions that satisfy the types without giving an actual argument for construction. Using the :t command, you can check the type of an expression, so as a result, you get:

```
1  Idris> :t A
2  A : Type -> Type -> Type
3  Idris> :t A_inst
4  A_inst : a -> b -> A a b
```

This shows the type definitions for the newly-defined type and its value constructor. Note how you created a product type here. Idris has a built-in[4] notion of pairs, which is a data type that can be defined in terms of products. For example, (1, 2) is one pair. You can also define tuples with (1, "Hi", True), which is equivalent to (1, ("Hi", True)). This is a pair where the first element is a number, and the second element is a pair. Note that the types (a, b) -> c (curried) and a -> b -> c (uncurried) represent the same thing.

Analogously, if you want to create a sum type, you can do the following:

```
1  data B a b = B_inst_left a | B_inst_right b
```

This is equivalent to:

```
1  data B : Type -> Type -> Type where
2      B_inst_left : a -> B a b
3      B_inst_right : b -> B a b
```

---

[4] By built-in, this usually means it's part of Idris' library. You can always implement it if you need to.

With either of these definitions in scope, you get:

```
1  Idris> :t B
2  B : Type -> Type -> Type
3  Idris> :t B_inst_left
4  B_inst_left : a -> B a b
5  Idris> :t B_inst_right
6  B_inst_right : b -> B a b
```

The B_inst_left and B_inst_right functions are also known as *introduction rules*. For extracting values from data types, such as B a b, also known as *elimination rules*, you can use pattern matching[5]. As an example, to extract a from B a b, you use the following function:

```
1  f : B a b -> a
2  f (B_inst_left a) = a
```

Note how you use the data type at the function type level and the value constructor in the function definition to pattern-match against.

Natural numbers can be defined as data Nat = Z | S Nat, where you either have a zero or a successor of a natural number. Note how this type is not polymorphic (it doesn't accept any variables after the type name). Natural numbers are built-in as a type in Idris.

You can use the operator == to compare two numbers. Note that == is still a function, but it's an infix one. This means that unlike other functions that you define which are *prefix* (they start at the beginning of the expression), == needs to appear between the parameters. For example:

---

[5] Although product and sum types are very general, due to polymorphism, you can say something very specific about the structure of their values. For instance, suppose you've defined a type like so: data C a b c = C_left a | C_right (b,c). A value of type C can only come into existence in one of two ways: as a value of the form C_left x for a value x : a, or as a value of the form C_right (y,z) for values y : b and z : c.

```
1  Idris> 1 == 1
2  True : Bool
```

Idris has several built-in primitive types, including: Bool, Char, List, String (list of characters), Integer, and so on. The only value constructors for the type Bool are True and False. The difference between a Nat and an Integer is that Integer can also contain negative values. Here are some examples of interacting with these types:

```
1   Idris> "Test"
2   "Test" : String
3   Idris> '!'
4   '!' : Char
5   Idris> 1
6   1 : Integer
7   Idris> '1'
8   '1' : Char
9   Idris> [1, 2, 3]
10  [1, 2, 3] : List Integer
```

Using the :doc command, you can get detailed information about a data type:

```
1  Idris> :doc Nat
2  Data type Prelude.Nat.Nat : Type
3      Natural numbers: unbounded, unsigned integers which can
        be pattern
4       matched.
5
6  Constructors:
7      Z : Nat
8           Zero
9
```

```
10      S : Nat -> Nat
11          Successor
```

In order to make Idris infer the necessary type of the function that needs to be built, you can take advantage of holes. A *hole* is any variable that starts with a question mark. For example, if you have the following definition:

```
1   test : Bool -> Bool
2   test p = ?hole1
```

You can ask Idris to tell you the type of hole1. That is, with :t hole1, you can see that Idris inferred that the specific result is expected to be of type Bool. This is useful because it allows you to write programs incrementally (piece by piece) instead of constructing the program all at once.

Exercise 3   Define your own custom type. One example is data Person = PersonInst String Nat, where String represents the person's name and Nat represents the person's age. Use the constructor to generate some objects of that type. Afterward, use :t to check the types of the type and value constructors.

Exercise 4   Come up with a function that works with your custom type (for example, it extracts some value) by pattern-matching against its value constructor(s).

Exercise 5   Repeat Exercise 4 and use holes to check the types of the expressions used in your function definition.

4.1.3. Anonymous Lambda Functions

With the let X in Y syntax, you're defining a set of variables X, which are only visible in the body of Y. As an example, here is one way to use this syntax:

```
1  Idris> let f = 1 in f
2  1 : Integer
```

Alternatively, the REPL has a command :let that allows you to set a variable without evaluating it right away, so that can be used at a later point:

```
1  Idris> :let f = 1
2  Idris> f
3  1 : Integer
```

❓What's the difference between **let and :let?**

let is an extension of the lambda calculus syntax. The expression let x = y in e is equivalent to (\x . e) y. It is useful since it makes it easy to shorten a lambda expression by factoring out common subexpressions.

:let is different in that it is used to bind new names at the top level of an interactive Idris session.

Lambda (anonymous) functions are defined with the \a, b, ..., n => .... syntax. For example:

```
1  Idris> let addThree = (\x, y, z => x + y + z) in
   addThree 1 2 3
2  6 : Integer
```

59

This example defines a function called addThree that accepts three parameters and as a result sums them. However, if you do not pass all parameters to a function, it will result in the following:

```
1  Idris> let addThree = (\x, y, z => x + y + z) in
   addThree 1 2
2  \z => prim addBigInt 3 z : Integer -> Integer
```

You can see (from the type) that as a result, you get another function.

ⓘDefinition 1   Currying is a concept that allows you to evaluate a function with multiple parameters as a sequence of functions, each having a single parameter.

Function application in Idris is left-associative (just like in lambda calculus), which means that if you try to evaluate addThree 1 2 3, it will be evaluated as (((addThree 1) 2) 3). A combination of left-associative functions and currying (i.e., partial evaluation of function) is what allows you to write addThree 1 2 3, which is much more readable.

Arrow types are right-associative (just like in lambda calculus), which means that addThree 1 : a -> a -> a is equivalent to addThree 1 : (a -> (a -> a)). If you had written a type of (a -> a) -> a instead, this function would accept as its first parameter a function that takes an a and returns an a, and then the original function also returns an a. This is how you define higher-order functions, which are discussed later. Note how a starts with a lowercase letter, thus it is a polymorphic type.

The if...then...else syntax is defined as follows:

```
1  Idris> if 1 == 1 then 'a' else 'b'
2  'a' : Char
3  Idris> if 2 == 1 then 'a' else 'b'
4  'b' : Char
```

✏ **Exercise 6**   Write a lambda function that returns True if the parameter passed to it is 42 and False otherwise.

4.1.4. Recursive Functions

By Definition 19 in Chapter 2, recursive functions are functions that refer to themselves. One example is the even : Nat -> Bool function, which determines whether a natural number is even. It can be defined as follows:

```
1  even : Nat -> Bool
2  even Z     = True
3  even (S k) = not (even k)
```

The definition states that 0 is an even number, and that n + 1 is even or not depending on the parity (evenness) of n. As a result, you get:

```
1  Idris> even 3
2  False : Bool
3  Idris> even 4
4  True : Bool
5  Idris> even 5
6  False : Bool
```

The way even 5 unfolds in Idris is as follows:

```
1  even 5 =
2  not (even 4) =
3  not (not (even 3)) =
4  not (not (not (even 2))) =
5  not (not (not (not (even 1)))) =
6  not (not (not (not (not (even 0))))) =
```

```
 7  not (not (not (not (not True)))) =
 8  not (not (not (not False))) =
 9  not (not (not True)) =
10  not (not False) =
11  not True =
12  False
```

This exhibits a recursive behavior since the recursive cases were reduced to the base case in an attempt to get a result. With this example, you can see the power of recursion and how it allows you to process values in a repeating manner.

A recursive function can generate an **iterative** or a **recursive** process:

- *An iterative process*[6] (tail recursion) is a process where the return value at any point in computation is captured completely by its parameters.

- A *recursive process,* in contrast, is one where the return value is not captured at any point in computation by the parameters, and so it relies on postponed evaluations.

In the previous example, even generates a recursive process since it needs to go down to the base case, and then build its way back up to do the calculations that were postponed. Alternatively, you can rewrite even so that it captures the return value by introducing another variable, as such:

```
1  even : Nat -> Bool -> Bool
2  even Z t     = t
3  even (S k) t = even k (not t)
```

---

[6]The key idea is not that a tail-recursive function *is* an iterative loop, but that a smart enough compiler can *pretend* that it is and evaluate it using constant function stack space.

In this case, you can refer to the return value of the function (second parameter) at any point in the computation. As a consequence, this function generates an iterative process, since the results are captured in the parameters. Note how this example brings down the base case to refer to the parameter, instead of a constant True. Here is how Idris evaluates even 5 True:

```
1   even 5 True =
2   even 4 False =
3   even 3 True =
4   even 2 False =
5   even 1 True =
6   even 0 False =
7   False
```

To conclude, iterative processes take fewer calculation steps and are usually more performant than recursive processes. Recursive functions, combined with pattern-matching, are one of the most powerful tools in Idris since they allow for computation. They are also useful for proving mathematical theorems with induction, as you will see in later examples.

 Exercise 7 Factorial is defined as:

$$fact(n) = \begin{cases} 1, \text{if } n = 0 \\ n \cdot fact(n-1), \text{otherwise} \end{cases}, \text{otherwise}$$

Unfold the evaluation of fact(5) on paper and then implement it in Idris and confirm that Idris also computes the same value.

Hint: The type is fact : Nat -> Nat and you should pattern-match against Z (Nat value constructor for 0) and (S n) (successor).

✏ **Exercise 8**   Rewrite the factorial function to generate an iterative process.

Hint: The type is `fact_iter : Nat -> Nat -> Nat` and you should pattern-match against `Z  acc` (number 0 and accumulator) and `(S  n)  acc` (successor and accumulator).

4.1.5. Recursive Data Types

You can think of type constructors as functions at the type level. Taking the concept of recursion to this context yields *recursive types*.

ⓘ **Definition 2**   A **recursive data type** is a data type where some of its constructors have a reference to the same data type.

Let's start by defining a recursive data type, which is a data type that in the constructor refers to itself. In fact, earlier in this book, we provided a recursive definition - `Nat`. As a motivating example, try to define the representation of lists. For this data type, you'll use a combination of sum and product types. A list is defined as either `End` (end of the list) or `Cons` (construct), which is a value appended to another `MyList`:

```
1   data MyList a = Cons a (MyList a) | End
```

This means that the `MyList` type has two constructors—`End` and `Cons`. If it's `End`, it's the end of the list (and does not accept any more values). However, if it's `Cons`, you need to append another value (e.g., `Cons  3`), and afterward, you have to specify another value of type `MyList  a` (which can be `End` or another `Cons`). This definition allows you to define a list. As an example, this is how you would represent (1, 2) using the Cons End representation:

```
1  Idris> :t Cons 1 (Cons 2 End)
2  Cons 1 (Cons 2 End) : MyList Integer
3  Idris> :t Cons 'a' (Cons 'b' End)
4  Cons 'a' (Cons 'b' End) : MyList Char
```

Note how Idris automatically infers the polymorphic type to MyList Integer and MyList Char. In particular, these lists are *homogeneous*; all the items in MyList a must have type a.

Here is one way of implementing the concatenation function, which given two lists, should produce a list with the elements appended:

```
1  add' : MyList a -> MyList a -> MyList a
2  add' End ys        = ys
3  add' (Cons x xs) ys = Cons x (add' xs ys)
```

The first line of the code says that add' is a function that accepts two polymorphic lists (MyList Nat, MyList Char, etc.) and produces the same list as a result. The second line of the code pattern-matches against the first list and when it's empty it returns the second list. The third line of the code also pattern-matches against the first list, but this time it covers the Cons case. So whenever there is a Cons in the first list, as a result, it returns this element Cons x appended recursively to add' xs ys, where xs is the remainder of the first list and ys is the second list. Here's an example:

```
1  Idris> add' (Cons 1 (Cons 2 (Cons 3 End))) (Cons 4 End)
2  Cons 1 (Cons 2 (Cons 3 (Cons 4 End))) : MyList Integer
```

✎ **Exercise 9** Unfold add' (Cons 1 (Cons 2 (Cons 3 End))) (Cons 4 End) on paper to get a better understanding of how this definition appends two lists.

✏️ **Exercise 10**   Come up with a definition for `length'`, which should return the number of elements, given a list.

Hint: The type is `length' : MyList a -> Nat`.

✏️ **Exercise 11**   Come up with a definition for `even_members`, which should return a new list with even natural numbers only.

Hint: The type is `even_members : MyList Nat -> MyList Nat`. You can reuse the definition of `even` discussed earlier.

✏️ **Exercise 12**   Come up with a definition for `sum'`, which should return a number that will be the sum of all elements in a list of natural numbers.

Hint: The type is `sum' : MyList Nat -> Nat`.

4.1.6. Total and Partial Functions

ℹ️ **Definition 3**   A **total function** is a function that terminates (or returns a value) for all possible inputs.

A partial function is the opposite of a total function. If a function is total, its type can be understood as a precise description of what that function can do. Idris differentiates total from partial functions but allows defining both.[7] As an example, if you assume that you have a function that returns a String, then:

1. If it's total, it will return a String in finite time.

2. If it's partial, unless it crashes or enters into an infinite loop, it will return a String.

In Idris, to define partial/total functions, you simply put the partial/total keyword in front of the function definition. For example, the following program defines two functions, test and test2, a partial and a total one, respectively:

```
1  partial
2  test : Nat -> String
3  test Z = "Hi"
4
5  total
6  test2 : Nat -> String
7  test2 Z = "Hi"
8  test2 _ = "Hello"
```

If you try to interact with these functions, you get the following results:

```
1  Idris> test 0
2  "Hi" : String
3  Idris> test 1
4  test 1 : String
5  Idris> test2 0
6  "Hi" : String
7  Idris> test2 1
8  "Hello" : String
```

---

[7] Partial (non-terminating) functions make Idris Turing complete.

Note that the evaluation of test 1 does not produce a computed value as a result. Note that at compile-time, Idris will **evaluate the types only for total functions**.

✎ **Exercise 13**   Try to define a function to be total and at the same time make sure you are not covering all input cases. Note what errors will Idris return in this case.

4.1.7. Higher-Order Functions

ⓘ**Definition 4**   A **higher-order function** takes one or more functions as parameters or returns a function as a result.

There are three built-in higher-order functions that are generally useful: map, filter, fold (left and right). Here's the description of each:

- map takes as input a function with a single parameter and a list and returns a list where all members in the list have this function applied to them.

- filter that takes as input a function (predicate) with a single parameter (that returns a Bool) and a list and only returns those members in the list whose predicate evaluates to True.

- fold takes as input a combining function that accepts two parameters (current value and accumulator), an initial value, and a list and returns a value combined with this function. There are two types of folds—a left and a right one—which combine from the left and the right, respectively.

Here's an example:

```
1  dris> map (\x => x + 1) [1, 2, 3]
2  [2, 3, 4] : List Integer
3  Idris> filter (\x => x > 1) [1, 2, 3]
4  [2, 3] : List Integer
5  Idris> foldl (\x, y => x + y) 0 [1, 2, 3]
6  6 : Integer
7  Idris> foldr (\x, y => x + y) 0 [1, 2, 3]
8  6 : Integer
```

You can implement the map function yourself:

```
1  mymap : (a -> a) -> List a -> List a
2  mymap _ []      = []
3  mymap f (x::xs) = (f x) :: (mymap f xs)
```

Note that :: is used by the built-in List type, and it is equivalent to Cons, which you saw earlier. However, since :: is an infix operator, it has to go between the two arguments. The [] value represents the empty list and is equivalent to End. In addition, the built-in List type is polymorphic.

✏️ **Exercise 14**   Run a few different calculations with mymap in order to get a deeper understanding of how it works.

✏️ **Exercise 15**   Implement a function called myfilter that acts just like the filter function.

Hint: Use :t filter to get its type.

Exercise 16   Given `foldl` `(\x, y => [y] ++ x) []`
`[1, 2, 3]` and `foldr` `(\x, y => y ++ [x]) [] [1, 2, 3]`:

1.   Evaluate both of them in Idris to see the values produced.

2.   Try to understand the differences between the two expressions.

3.   Remove the square brackets [and] in the lambda body to see what errors Idris produces.

4.   Evaluate the expressions on paper to figure out why they produce the given results.

4.1.8. Dependent Types

This section shows you how to implement the `List n` data type discussed in Section 3.3, which should limit the length of a list at the type level. Idris has a built-in list like this called `Vect`, so to avoid any conflicts, this example calls it `MyVect`. You can implement it as follows:

```
1  data MyVect : (n : Nat) -> Type where
2      Empty : MyVect 0
3      Cons : (x : Nat) -> (xs : MyVect len) -> MyVect (S len)
```

This example creates a new type called `MyVect`, which accepts a natural number n and returns a `Type` that is joined with two value constructors:

1.   `Empty`, which is just the empty vector (list).

2.   `Cons : (x : Nat) -> (xs : MyVect len) -> MyVect (S len)`, which, given a natural number x and a vector xs of length `len`, will return a vector of length S `len`—that is, `len + 1`.

Note how this example additionally specified names to the parameters (n : Nat, xs : MyVect len, etc.). This can be useful when you want to reference those parameters elsewhere in the type definition.

If you now run the following code snippet, it will pass the compile-time checks:

```
1   x : MyVect 2
2   x = Cons 1 (Cons 2 Empty)
```

However, if you try to run this code snippet instead:

```
1   x : MyVect 3
2   x = Cons 1 (Cons 2 Empty)
```

you will get the following error:

```
1   Type mismatch between
2       MyVect 0 (Type of Empty)
3   and
4       MyVect 1 (Expected type)
```

Idris is telling you that your types do not match and that it cannot verify the "proof" you provided.

This example implemented a dependent type that puts the length of a list at the type level. In programming languages that do not support dependent types, this is usually checked at the code level (runtime) and compile-time checks are not able to verify this.

One example where such a guarantee might be useful is in preventing buffer overflows. You could encode the dimension of an array at the type level and statically guarantee that array reads and writes only happen within bounds.

✎ Exercise 17   Come up with a function called `isSingleton` that accepts a `Bool` and returns a `Type`. This function should return an object of type `Nat` in the `True` case and `MyVect Nat` otherwise. Further, implement a function called `mkSingle` that accepts a `Bool` and returns `isSingleton True` or `isSingleton False`, and as a computed value, returns 0 or `Empty`.

Hint: The data definitions are `isSingleton : Bool -> Type` and `mkSingle : (x : Bool) -> isSingleton x`, respectively.

4.1.9. Implicit Parameters

Implicit parameters (arguments) allow you to bring values from the type level to the program level. At the program level, by using curly braces, you allow them to be used in the definition of the function. Consider the following example, which uses the dependent type `MyVect` defined earlier:

```
1  lengthMyVect : MyVect n -> Nat
2  lengthMyVect {n = k} list = k
```

This example defines a function called `lengthMyVect` that takes a `MyVect` and returns a natural number. The n value in the definition of the function will be the same as the value of n at the type level. They are called *implicit parameters* because the caller of this function needn't pass these parameters. In the function definition, you define implicit parameters with curly braces and specify the list parameter, which is of type `MyVect` n, to pattern-match against it. Note how this example doesn't refer to the list parameter in the computation part of this function. Instead, you can use an underscore (which represents an unused parameter) to get the following:

```
1  lengthMyVect : MyVect n -> Nat
2  lengthMyVect {n = k} _ = k
```

You can also have implicit parameters at the type level. As a matter of fact, an equivalent type definition of that function is as follows:

```
1  lengthMyVect : {n : Nat} -> MyVect n -> Nat
```

If you ask Idris to give you the type of this function, you will get the following for either of these type definitions:

```
1  Idris> :t lengthMyVect
2  lengthMyVect : MyVect n -> Nat
```

However, you can use the :set showimplicits command, which will show the implicits on the type level. If you do that, you will get the following for either of the type definitions:

```
1  Idris> :set showimplicits
2  Idris> :t lengthMyVect
3  lengthMyVect : {n : Nat} -> MyVect n -> Nat
```

To pass values for implicit arguments, use the following syntax:

```
1  Idris> lengthMyVect {n = 1} (Cons 1 Empty)
2  1 : Nat
```

✎ **Exercise 18**   Try to evaluate the following code and observe the results:

```
1  lengthMyVect {n = 2} (Cons 1 Empty)
```

4.1.10. Pattern-Matching Expressions

You've seen how pattern matching is a powerful concept, in that it allows you to pattern-match against value constructors. For example, you can write a filtering function that, given a list of naturals, produces a list of even naturals by reusing the earlier definition of even:

```
1  total even_members : MyList Nat -> MyList Nat
2  even_members End         = End
3  even_members (Cons x l') = if (even x)
4                               then (Cons x (even_members l'))
5                               else even_members l'
```

This function is a recursive one, and depending on the value of even x, it will branch the recursion. Since pattern matching works against value constructors, and even x is a function call, you can't easily pattern-match against it. You use even x in the function body to do this check. Idris provides another keyword called with, which allows you to pattern-match a value of some expression. The with keyword has the following syntax:

```
1  function (pattern_match_1) with (expression)
2    pattern_match_1' | (value of expression to match) = ...
3    pattern_match_2' | (value of expression to match) = ...
4    ...
```

Note how you have to specify new pattern-matching clauses after the line that uses the with keyword. This is so you won't have the original pattern-match in context. Given this, an alternative definition of this function is as follows:

```
1  total even_members' : MyList Nat -> MyList Nat
2  even_members' End = End
3  even_members' (Cons x l') with (even x)
4    even_members' (Cons x l') | True = Cons x (even_members' l')
5    even_members' (Cons _ l') | False = (even_members' l')
```

This function defines two new pattern matches after the line that uses the `with` keyword. Since you don't have x and l' in this new pattern-matching context, you have to rewrite them on the left side of the pipe. On the right side of the pipe, you pattern-match against the value of even x, and then branch the recursion (computation).

4.1.11. Interfaces and Implementations

Interfaces are defined using the `interface` keyword; they allow you to add constraints to types that implement them.[8] As an example, consider the Eq interface:

```
1   interface Eq a where
2        (==) : a -> a -> Bool
3        (/=) : a -> a -> Bool
4        -- Minimal complete definition:
5        --      (==) or (/=)
6      x /= y = not (x == y)
7      x == y = not (x /= y)
```

Note how you can specify comments in the code by using two dashes. Comments are ignored by the Idris compiler and are only useful to the reader of the code.

The definition says that, for a type to implement the Eq interface, there must be an implementation of the functions == and /= for that specific type. Additionally, the interface also contains definitions for the functions, but this is optional. Since the definition of == depends on /= (and vice versa), it will be sufficient to provide only one of them in the implementation; the other one will be automatically generated.

---

[8] They are equivalent to Haskell's `class` keyword. Interfaces in Idris are very similar to OOP's interfaces.

As an example, assume that you have a data type:

```
1  data Foo : Type where
2      Fooinst : Nat -> String -> Foo
```

To implement Eq for Foo, you can use the following code:

```
1  implementation Eq Foo where
2      (Fooinst x1 str1) ==
3          (Fooinst x2 str2) = (x1 == x2) && (str1 == str2)
```

The example uses == for Nat and String, since this is defined in Idris. With this, you can easily use == and /= on Fooinst:

```
1  Idris> Fooinst 3 "orange" == Fooinst 6 "apple"
2  False : Bool
3  Idris> Fooinst 3 "orange" /= Fooinst 6 "apple"
4  True : Bool
```

The Nats implement the built-in Num interface, which is what allows you to use 0 and Z interchangeably.

Exercise 19   Implement your own data type called Person that accepts a person's name and age, and then implement an interface for comparing Persons.

Hint: One valid data type is data Person = Personinst String Int.

4.2. Curry-Howard Isomorphism

The *Curry-Howard isomorphism* (also known as Curry-Howard correspondence) is the direct relationship between computer programs and mathematical proofs. It is named after the mathematician Haskell Curry and logician William Howard. A mathematical proof is represented by a computer program and the formula that you prove is the type of that program. As an example, consider at the swap function, which is defined as follows:

```
1   swap : (a, b) -> (b, a)
2   swap (a, b) = (b, a)
```

The isomorphism says that this function has an equivalent form of mathematical proof. Although it may not be immediately obvious, consider the following proof: Given P ∧ Q, prove that Q ∧ P. In order to prove it, you have to use the inference rules *and-introduction* and *and-elimination,* which are defined as follows:

1. And-introduction means that if you are given P, Q, you can construct a proof for P ∧ Q.

2. Left and-elimination means that if you are given P ∧ Q, you can conclude P.

3. Right and-elimination means that if you are given P ∧ Q, you can conclude Q.

If you want to implement this proof in Idris, you can represent it as a product type as follows:

```
1   data And a b = And_intro a b
2
3   and_comm : And a b -> And b a
4   and_comm (And_intro a b) = And_intro b a
```

As discussed, you can use product types to encode pairs. Note the following similarities with the earlier definition of swap:

1. And_intro x y is equivalent to constructing a product type (x, y).

2. Left-elimination, which is a pattern match of And_intro a _, is equivalent to the first element of the product type.

3. Right-elimination, which is a pattern match of And_intro _ b, is equivalent to the second element of the product type.

As long as Idris' type checker terminates, you can be certain that the program provides a mathematical proof of its type. This is why Idris' type checker only evaluates total functions, to keep the type checking decidable.

4.3. Quantitative Type Theory

This book was written using Idris 1; however, Idris 2 was released in 2020 and it's based on **Quantitative Type Theory**. Most of the examples in this book should be compatible with Idris 2. However, some Idris 2 code will not be compatible with Idris 1. Idris 2 is recommended, as it also might contain some bug fixes.

Quantitative type theory gives more computational power at the type level. It allows you to specify a quantity for each variable:

- 0, means that the variable is not used at runtime.

- 1, which means that the variable is used only once at runtime.

- Unrestricted (default), which is the same behavior as in Idris 1.

Consider the lengthMyVect example again. If you change its definition from k to k + k, the type checker will not complain:

```
1  lengthMyVect : {n : Nat} -> MyVect n -> Nat
2  lengthMyVect {n = k} _ = k + k
```

However, if you specify that the variable n can be used only once:

```
1  lengthMyVect : {1 n : Nat} -> MyVect n -> Nat
```

Then the type checker will throw an error for k + k, but not for k.

CHAPTER 5

Proving in Idris

This chapter provides several examples to demonstrate the power of Idris. It includes mathematical proofs. There are a lot of Idris built-ins that help you achieve your goals. Each section introduces the relevant definitions.

ⓘ Definition 1   The **equality data type** is roughly defined as follows:

```
1  data (=) : a -> b -> Type where
2  Refl : x = x
```

You can use the Refl value constructor to prove equalities.

ⓘ Definition 2   The **the** function accepts A : Type and value : A and returns value : A. You can use it to manually assign a type to an expression.

✎ Exercise 1   Check the documentation of the equality type with :doc (=).

© Boro Sitnikovski 2023
B. Sitnikovski, *Introduction to Dependent Types with Idris*,
https://doi.org/10.1007/978-1-4842-9259-4_5

✎ **Exercise 2**   Evaluate the Nat 3 and the Integer 3 and note the differences. Afterward, try to implement the ' so that it will act just like the and test the previous evaluations again.

✎ **Exercise 3**   Given data Or a b = Or_introl a | Or_intror b, show that a → (a ∨ b) and b → (a ∨ b). Afterward, check the documentation of the built-in Either and compare it to the Or.

Hint:

```
1  proof_1 : a -> Or a b
2  proof_1 a = Or_introl ?prf
```

✎ **Exercise 4**   In Section 4.2, you implemented And. How does it compare to the built-in Pair?

5.1. Weekdays

This section introduces a way to represent weekdays and then do some proofs with them. Start with the following data structure:

```
1  data Weekday = Mon | Tue | Wed | Thu | Fri | Sat | Sun
```

The Weekday type has seven value constructors, one for each day. The data type and its constructors do not accept any parameters.

5.1.1. First Proof (Auto-Inference)

This example proves that after Monday comes Tuesday. Start by implementing a function that, given a day, returns the next day:

```
1   total next_day : Weekday -> Weekday
2   next_day Mon = Tue
3   next_day Tue = Wed
4   next_day Wed = Thu
5   next_day Thu = Fri
6   next_day Fri = Sat
7   next_day Sat = Sun
8   next_day Sun = Mon
```

Given these definitions, you can write the proof as follows:

```
1   our_first_proof : next_day Mon = Tue
2   our_first_proof = ?prf
```

This example uses the function next_day Mon = Tue at the type level, for the type of our_first_proof. Since next_day is total, Idris will be able to evaluate next_day Mon at compile-time. This example uses a hole for the definition since you still don't know what the proof will look like. If you run this code in Idris, it will tell you that you have a hole called prf to fill:

```
1   Type checking ./first_proof.idr
2   Holes: Main.prf
3   Idris> :t prf
4   ----------------------------------------
5   prf : Tue = Tue
```

If you check the type of prf, you'll notice how Idris evaluated the left part of the equation at compile-time. In order to prove that Tue = Tue, you can just use Refl:

```
1  our_first_proof : next_day Mon = Tue
2  our_first_proof = Refl
```

Reload the file in Idris:

```
1  Idris> :r
2  Type checking ./first_proof.idr
```

The type check was successful. Per the Curry-Howard isomorphism, this means that you've successfully proven that next_day Mon = Tue. So, after Monday comes Tuesday!

Exercise 5   Remove one or more of the pattern-match definitions of next_day and observe the error that Idris produces. Afterward, alter the function so that it is not total anymore and observe the results.

Exercise 6   Implement prev_day and prove that Sunday comes before Monday.

5.1.2. Second Proof (Rewrite)

In addition to the previous proof, this example implements a function that accepts a Weekday and returns True if it's Monday and False otherwise.

```
1  is_it_monday : Weekday -> Bool
2  is_it_monday Mon = True
3  is_it_monday _   = False
```

For the sake of example, let's prove that for any given day, if it's Monday, then is_it_monday will return True. It's obvious from the definition of is_it_monday, but proving that is a whole different story. The type definition that you need to prove is as follows:

```
1  our_second_proof : (day : Weekday) -> day = Mon ->
2      is_it_monday day = True
```

The first parameter is called day : Weekday, so you can refer to it in the type definition. The second parameter says that day = Mon and the return value is is_it_monday day = True. You can treat the first and second parameters as givens, since you are allowed to assume them (per the definition of implication). With that, you can proceed to the function definition:

```
1  our_second_proof day day_eq_Mon = Refl
```

In this definition, day and day_eq_Mon are assumptions (givens). If you run this code in Idris, it will produce an error at compile-time since it cannot deduce that True is equal to is_it_monday day. In the previous proof example, Idris could infer everything from the definitions at compile-time. However, at this point, you need to help Idris do the inference since it cannot derive the proof based only on the definitions. You can change the Refl to a hole prf:

```
1      day : Weekday
2      day_eq_Mon : day = Mon
3  --------------------------------------
4  prf : is_it_monday day = True
```

Note how checking the type of the hole lists the givens/premises (above the separator) and the goal(s) (below the separator). Along with prf, you also get day and day_eq_Mon in the list of givens, per the left side of the function definition of our_second_proof.

? How do you replace something you have in the givens with the goal?

If you only had a way to tell Idris that it needs to replace day with day = Mon to get to is_it_monday Mon = True, it could infer the rest.

ⓘ Definition 3   The **rewrite** keyword can be used to rewrite expressions. If you have X : x = y, the syntax rewrite X in Y will replace all occurrences of x with y in Y.

With the power to do rewrites, you can attempt the following proof:

```
1  our_second_proof : (day : Weekday) -> day = Mon ->
2      is_it_monday day = True
3  our_second_proof day day_eq_Mon = rewrite day_eq_Mon in ?prf
```

Idris produces:

```
1  Idris> :t prf
2    day : Weekday
3    day_eq_Mon : day = Mon
4    _rewrite_rule : day = Mon
5  --------------------------------------
6  prf : True = True
```

Changing prf to Refl completes the proof. You just proved that $\forall x \in$ Weekdays, x = Mon $\rightarrow$ IsItMonday(x). This example assumed x = Mon is true (by pattern matching against day_eq_Mon in the definition) and then used rewriting to alter x.

✎ **Exercise 7**   Implement the is_it_sunday function, which returns True if the given day is Sunday and False otherwise.

✎ **Exercise 8**   Prove the following formula in Idris: ∀ x ∈ Weekdays, x = Sun → IsItSunday(x).

5.1.3. Third Proof (Impossible)

This section proves that is_it_monday Tue = True is a contradiction.

Per intuitionistic logic, in order to prove that P is a contradiction, you need to prove P → ⊥. Idris provides an empty data type called Void. This data type has no value constructors (proofs) for it.

To prove that is_it_monday Tue = True is a contradiction, do the following:

```
1  our_third_proof : is_it_monday Tue = True -> Void
2  our_third_proof mon_is_Tue = ?prf
```

Check the type of the hole:

```
1    mon_is_Tue : False = True
2  ---------------------------------------
3  prf : Void
```

❓ How do you prove prf, given that there are no value constructors for Void?

It seems that at this point you are stuck. You need to find a way to tell Idris that this proof is impossible.

> **ⓘ Definition 4**   The **impossible** keyword can be used to prove statements that are not true. With this keyword, you say that proof for a data type cannot be constructed, since a value constructor for that particular type does not exist.

Let's slightly rewrite the function:

```
1  our_third_proof : is_it_monday Tue = True -> Void
2  our_third_proof Refl impossible
```

With this syntax, you're telling Idris that the reflexivity of False = True is impossible and thus the proof is complete.

> **✎ Exercise 9**   Check the documentation of Void and try to implement Void' yourself. Rewrite the previous proof to use Void' instead of Void.

> **✎ Exercise 10**   Prove that 1 = 2 is a contradiction.
>
> Hint: The type is 1 = 2 -> Void.

5.2. Natural Numbers

This section shows you how to prove facts about natural numbers and does some induction. Recall that a natural number is defined either as 0 or as the successor of a natural number. So, 0, S 0, S (S 0), ... are the first natural numbers. Start with the following definitions:

```
1  data MyNat = Zero | Succ MyNat
2
3  total mynat_plus : MyNat -> MyNat -> MyNat
4  mynat_plus Zero     m = m
5  mynat_plus (Succ k) m = Succ (mynat_plus k m)
```

Note how the definition of MyNat is recursive compared to Weekday. A consequence of that is that you may need to use induction for some proofs.

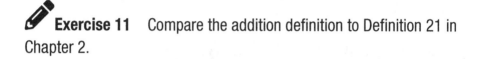 **Exercise 11**   Compare the addition definition to Definition 21 in Chapter 2.

5.2.1. First Proof (Auto-Inference and Existence)

In this section, you'll see how to prove that 0 + a = a, given the definitions for natural numbers and addition.

For that, you need to implement a function that accepts a natural number a and returns the proposition that mynat_plus Zero a = a.

```
1  total our_first_proof_inf : (a : MyNat) -> mynat_plus
   Zero a = a
2  our_first_proof_inf a = ?prf
```

If you check the type of the hole, you get that the goal is prf : a = a, so changing the hole to a Refl completes the proof. Idris can automatically infer the proof by directly substituting definitions.

To prove the existence of a successor, that is, Succ x, per intuitionistic logic, you need to construct a pair where the first element is x : MyNat and the second element is Succ x : MyNat. Idris has a built-in data structure for constructing dependent pairs, called DPair.

```
1  total our_first_proof_exist : MyNat -> DPair MyNat
   (\_ => MyNat)
2  our_first_proof_exist x = MkDPair x (Succ x)
```

You just proved that $\exists x \in$ MyNat, Succ(x).

✏️ **Exercise 12**   Check the documentation of DPair and MkDPair and try to construct some dependent pairs.

5.2.2. Second Proof (Introduction of a New Given)

An alternative way to prove that a natural number exists is as follows:

```
1  total our_second_proof : MyNat
2  our_second_proof = ?prf
```

If you check the type of the hole, you get the following:

```
1  Holes: Main.prf
2  Idris> :t prf
3  ----------------------------------------
4  prf : MyNat
```

❓ By the definition of MyNat, you know that a value constructor of MyNat exists. But how do you tell Idris?

ℹ️ **Definition 5**   The **let** keyword introduced earlier allows you to add a new given to the list of hypotheses.

Slightly rewrite the code as follows:

```
1  total our_second_proof : MyNat
2  our_second_proof = let the_number = Zero in ?prf
```

Check the type:

```
1    the_number : MyNat
2  ----------------------------------------
3  prf : MyNat
```

Changing prf to the_number concludes the proof.

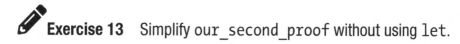

Exercise 13   Simplify our_second_proof without using let.

Hint: Providing a valid value constructor that satisfies (inhabits) the type is a constructive proof.

Exercise 14   Construct a proof similar to our_second_proof without defining a function for it and by using the the function.

5.2.3. Third Proof (Induction)

This section shows you how to prove that a + 0 = a. You could try to use the same approach as in Section 5.2.1:

```
1  total our_third_proof : (a : MyNat) -> mynat_plus a Zero = a
2  our_third_proof a = Refl
```

If you try to run this code, Idris will produce an error saying that there is a type mismatch between a and mynat_plus a Zero.

❓ It seems that you have just about all the definitions you need, but you're missing a piece. How do you reuse the definitions?

To prove that $a + 0 = a$, you can use mathematical induction, starting with the definitions you already have as the base case, and build on top of them until a + 0 = a. That is, you need to prove that 0 + 0 = 0 → (a - a) + 0 = a - a → ... → (a - 1) + 0 = a - 1 → a + 0 = a.

From here, rewrite the function to contain a base case and an inductive step:

```
1  total our_third_proof : (a : MyNat) -> mynat_plus a Zero = a
2  our_third_proof Zero     = ?base
3  our_third_proof (Succ k) = ?ind_hypothesis
```

Note how this example uses pattern matching against the definition of natural numbers. Pattern matching is similar to using proof by cases. Check the types of the holes:

```
1  Holes: Main.ind_hypothesis, Main.base
2  Idris> :t base
3  ---------------------------------------
4  base : Zero = Zero
5  Idris> :t ind_hypothesis
6    k : MyNat
7  ---------------------------------------
8  ind_hypothesis : Succ (mynat_plus k Zero) = Succ k
```

For the base case, you can just use Refl, but for the inductive step, you need to do something different. You need to find a way to assume (add to list of givens) a + 0 = a and show that (a+1)+0 = a+1 follows from that assumption. Since you pattern match on Succ k, you can use recursion on k along with let to generate the hypothesis:

```
1  total our_third_proof : (a : MyNat) -> mynat_plus a Zero = a
2  our_third_proof Zero      = Refl
3  our_third_proof (Succ k) = let ind_hypothesis = our_third_
   proof k in
4                                      ?conclusion
```

The proof givens and goals become:

```
1    k : MyNat
2    ind_hypothesis : mynat_plus k Zero = k
3  -------------------------------------
4  conclusion : Succ (mynat_plus k Zero) = Succ k
```

To prove the conclusion, simply rewrite the inductive hypothesis in the goal and you are done.

```
1  total our_third_proof : (a : MyNat) -> mynat_plus a Zero = a
2  our_third_proof Zero      = Refl
3  our_third_proof (Succ k) = let ind_hypothesis = our_third_
   proof k in
4                                      rewrite ind_hypothesis in
5                                      Refl
```

This concludes the proof.

Exercise 15   Observe the similarity between this proof and the proof in Section 2.3.4.

5.2.4. Ordering

Idris 1 has a built-in data type to order natural numbers, called LTE, which stands for less than or equal to. This data type has two constructors:

1. LTEZero is used to prove that 0 is less than or equal to any natural number.

2. LTESucc is used to prove that a ≤ b → S(a) ≤ S(b).

If you check the type of LTEZero, you get the following:

```
1 Idris> :t LTEZero
2 LTEZero : LTE 0 right
```

LTEZero does not accept any arguments, but you can pass right at the type level. With the use of implicits, you can construct a very simple proof to show that 0 ≤ 1:

```
1 Idris> LTEZero {right = S Z}
2 LTEZero : LTE 0 1
```

Similarly, with LTESucc, you can do the same:

```
1 Idris> LTESucc {left = Z} {right = S Z}
2 LTESucc : LTE 0 1 -> LTE 1 2
```

✐ **Exercise 16**   Check the documentation of GTE and then evaluate GTE 2 2. Observe what Idris returns and think about how GTE can be implemented in terms of LTE.

✐ **Exercise 17**   This example used the built-in type LTE, which is defined for Nat. Try to come up with an LTE definition for MyNat.

5.2.5. Safe Division

Idris 1 provides a function called divNat that divides two numbers. Check the documentation:

```
1  Idris> :doc divNat
2  Prelude.Nat.divNat : Nat -> Nat -> Nat
3
4      The function is not total as there are missing cases
```

Try to use it a couple of times:

```
1  Idris> divNat 4 2
2  2 : Nat
3  Idris> divNat 4 1
4  4 : Nat
5  Idris> divNat 4 0
6  divNat 4 0 : Nat
```

As expected, partial functions do not cover all inputs and thus divNat does not return a computed value when you divide by zero.

 How do you make a function like divNat total?

The only way to make this work is to pass a proof to divNat that says that the divisor is not 0. Idris has a built-in function for that, called divNatNZ.

You can check the documentation of this function as follows:

```
1  Idris> :doc divNatNZ ·
2  Prelude.Nat.divNatNZ : Nat -> (y : Nat) -> Not (y = 0) -> Nat
3      Division where the divisor is not zero.
4      The function is Total
```

This function is total, but you need to also provide a parameter to prove that the divisor is not zero. Fortunately, Idris 1 also provides a function called SIsNotZ, which accepts any natural number (through implicit argument x) and returns a proof that x + 1 is not zero.

Try to construct a few proofs:

```
1  Idris> SIsNotZ {x = 0}
2  SIsNotZ : (1 = 0) -> Void
3  Idris> SIsNotZ {x = 1}
4  SIsNotZ : (2 = 0) -> Void
5  Idris> SIsNotZ {x = 2}
6  SIsNotZ : (3 = 0) -> Void
```

Great. It seems that you have everything you need. You can safely divide as follows:

```
1  Idris> divNatNZ 4 2 (SIsNotZ {x = 1})
2  2 : Nat
3  Idris> divNatNZ 4 1 (SIsNotZ {x = 0})
4  4 : Nat
5  Idris> divNatNZ 4 0 (SIsNotZ {x = ???})
6  4 : Nat
```

You cannot construct a proof for the third case and so it will never be able to divide by zero, which is not allowed anyway.

✏️ **Exercise 18**   Implement SuccIsNotZ for MyNat, which works similarly to SIsNotZ.

✏️ **Exercise 19**   Implement minus and lte (and optionally div) for MyNat.

5.2.6. Maximum of Two Numbers

ⓘ **Definition 6**   The **maximum** of two numbers a and b is defined as:

$$max(a,b) = \begin{cases} b, \text{if } a \leq b \\ a, \text{otherwise} \end{cases}$$

This section tries to prove that a ≤ b → b = max(a, b). Idris 1 has a built-in function called maximum, so you can use that. Next, you need to figure out the type of the function to approach the proof. Intuitively, you might try the following:

```
1  our_proof : (a : Nat) -> (b : Nat) -> a <= b ->
   maximum a b = b
2  our_proof a b a_lt_b = ?prf
```

However, this won't work since a `<=` b is a Bool (per the `<=` function), not a Type. At the type level, you need to rely on LTE, which is a Type.

```
1  our_proof : (a : Nat) -> (b : Nat) -> LTE a b ->
   maximum a b = b
2  our_proof a b a_lt_b = ?prf
```

This compiles, so you have to figure out the hole. If you check its type, you get the following:

```
1    a : Nat
2    b : Nat
3    a_lt_b : LTE a b
4    --------------------------------------
5  prf : maximum a b = b
```

This looks a bit complicated, so you can further simplify by breaking the proof into several cases, by adding pattern matching for all combinations of the parameters' value constructors:

```
1  our_proof : (a : Nat) -> (b : Nat) -> LTE a b ->
   maximum a b = b
2  our_proof Z Z _                = Refl
3  our_proof Z (S k) _            = Refl
4  our_proof (S k) (S j) a_lt_b = ?prf
```

You get the following:

```
1    k : Nat
2    j : Nat
3    a_lt_b : LTE (S k) (S j)
4  --------------------------------------
5  prf : S (maximum k j) = S j
```

It seems like you have made progress, as this gives you something to work with. You can use induction on k and j and use a hole for the third parameter to ask Idris what type you need to satisfy:

```
1  our_proof : (a : Nat) -> (b : Nat) -> LTE a b ->
   maximum a b = b
2  our_proof Z Z _                = Refl
3  our_proof Z (S k) _            = Refl
4  our_proof (S k) (S j) a_lt_b = let IH = (our_proof
   k j ?prf) in
5                                 rewrite IH in
6                                 Refl
```

The hole produces the following:

```
1  Holes: Main.prf
2  Idris> :t prf
3    k : Nat
4    j : Nat
5    a_lt_b : LTE (S k) (S j)
6  -------------------------------------
7  prf : LTE k j
```

 How do you go from S(a) ≤ S(b) → a ≤ b?

It seems pretty obvious that, if you know that 1 ≤ 2, then also 0 ≤ 1, but you still need to find out how to tell Idris that this is true. Idris has a built-in function called fromLteSucc:

```
1  Idris> :doc fromLteSucc

2  Prelude.Nat.fromLteSucc : LTE (S m) (S n)
   -> LTE m n

3  If two numbers are ordered, their
   predecessors are too
```

It seems you have everything you need to conclude this proof. You can proceed as follows:

```
1  total
2  our_proof : (a : Nat) -> (b : Nat) -> LTE a b ->
   maximum a b = b
3  our_proof Z Z _              = Refl
4  our_proof Z (S k) _          = Refl
```

```
5  our_proof (S k) (S j) a_lt_b = let fls = fromLteSucc
   a_lt_b in
6                                  let IH = (our_proof k
                                   j fls) in
7                                  rewrite IH in
8                                  Refl
```

A more simplified version is as follows:

```
1  total
2  our_proof : (a : Nat) -> (b : Nat) -> LTE a b ->
   maximum a b = b
3  our_proof Z Z _              = Refl
4  our_proof Z (S k) _          = Refl
5  our_proof (S k) (S j) a_lt_b = rewrite
6                                 (our_proof k j (fromLteSucc
                                   a_lt_b)) in
7                                 Refl
```

🖉 **Exercise 20**   Use fromLteSucc with implicits to construct some proofs.

5.2.7. List of Even Naturals

This section shows you how to prove that a list of even numbers contains no odd numbers. You will reuse the even functions in Section 4.1.4 and even_members in Section 4.1.11. You also need another function to check if a list has odd numbers:

```
1  total has_odd : MyList Nat -> Bool
2  has_odd End         = False
3  has_odd (Cons x l') = if (even x) then has_odd l' else True
```

To prove that a list of even numbers contains no odd numbers, you can use the following type definition:

```
1  even_members_list_only_even : (l : MyList Nat) ->
2      has_odd (even_members l) = False
```

Note that has_odd is a branching computation depending on the value of even x, so you have to pattern-match with the value of expressions by using the with keyword. The base case is simply Refl:

```
1  even_members_list_only_even End = Refl
```

However, for the inductive step, you will use with on even n and produce proof depending on the evenness of the number:

```
1  even_members_list_only_even (Cons n l') with (even n)
   proof even_n
2    even_members_list_only_even (Cons n l') | False =
3        let IH = even_members_list_only_even l' in ?a
4    even_members_list_only_even (Cons n l') | True =
5        let IH = even_members_list_only_even l' in ?b
```

Note how you specify proof even_n right after the expression in the with match. The proof keyword followed by a variable brings you the proof of the expression to the list of premises. The with (even n) proof even_n expression will pattern-match on the results of even n and will also bring the even n proof in the premises. If you now check the first hole:

```
1   n : Nat
2   l' : MyList Nat
3   even_n : False = even n
4   IH : has_odd (even_members l') = False
5   -------------------------------------
6  a : has_odd (even_members l') = False
```

That should be simple; you can just use IH to solve the goal. For the second hole, you have:

```
1   n : Nat
2   l' : MyList Nat
3   even_n : True = even n
4   IH : has_odd (even_members l') = False
5   --------------------------------------
6   b : ifThenElse (even n) (has_odd (even_members l'))
7      True = False
```

? How do you rewrite the inductive hypothesis to the goal in this case?

It seems that you can't just rewrite here, since even_n has the order of the equality reversed. Idris provides a function called sym, which takes an equality of a = b and converts it to b = a.

You can try to rewrite sym even_n to the goal, so it now becomes:

```
1   n : Nat
2   l' : MyList Nat
3   even_n : True = even n
4   IH : has_odd (even_members l') = False
5   _rewrite_rule : even n = True
6   --------------------------------------
7   b : has_odd (even_members l') = False
```

As before, use IH to solve the goal. Thus, the complete proof is as follows:

```
1   even_members_list_only_even : (l : MyList Nat) ->
2       has_odd (even_members l) = False
3   even_members_list_only_even End = Refl
4   even_members_list_only_even (Cons n l') with (even n)
    proof even_n
5     even_members_list_only_even (Cons n l') | False =
6         let IH = even_members_list_only_even l' in IH
7     even_members_list_only_even (Cons n l') | True =
8         let IH = even_members_list_only_even l' in
9         rewrite sym even_n in IH
```

? How did mathematical induction work in this case?

Mathematical induction is defined in terms of natural numbers, but in this case, you used induction to prove a fact about a list. This works because you used a more general induction, called **structural induction**. Structural induction is used to prove that some proposition P(x) holds for all x of some sort of recursively defined data structure. For example, for lists, you used End as the base case and Cons as the inductive step. Thus, mathematical induction is a special case of structural induction for the Nat type.

✎ **Exercise 21**   Rewrite has_odd to use with in the recursive case and then repeat the previous proof.

5.2.8. Partial Orders

ⓘ **Definition 7**   A **binary relation** R on some set S is a partial order if the following properties are satisfied:

1. $\forall a \in S,$ aRa, that is, reflexivity

2. $\forall a, b, c \in S,$ aRb $\wedge$ bRc $\rightarrow$ aRc, that is, transitivity

3. $\forall a, b \in S,$ aRb $\wedge$ bRa $\rightarrow a = b$, that is, antisymmetry

---

Abstract this in Idris as an `interface`:

```
1  interface Porder (a : Type) (Order : a -> a -> Type) |
   Order where
2      total proofR : Order n n -- reflexivity
3      total proofT : Order n m -> Order m p -> Order n p --
       transitivity
4      total proofA : Order n m -> Order m n -> n = m --
       antisymmetry
```

The Porder interface accepts a Type and an Order relation, which is a built-in binary function in Idris 1. Since the interface has more than two parameters, you specify that Order is a determining parameter, that is, the parameter used to resolve the instance.

Now that you have an abstract interface, you can build a concrete implementation for it:

```
1  implementation Porder Nat LTE where
2      proofR {n = Z}   =
3          LTEZero
4      proofR {n = S _} =
```

```
5          LTESucc proofR
6
7      proofT LTEZero                              =
8          LTEZero
9      proofT (LTESucc n_lte_m) (LTESucc m_lte_p) =
10         LTESucc (proofT n_lte_m m_lte_p)
11
12     proofA LTEZero           LTEZero            =
13         Refl
14     proofA (LTESucc n_lte_m) (LTESucc m_lte_n) =
15         let IH = proofA n_lte_m m_lte_n in rewrite
           IH in Refl
```

You proved that the binary operation "less than or equal to" for Nats make a Porder. Interfaces allow you to group one or more functions so when you implement a specific interface, it's guaranteed to implement all such functions.

✎ **Exercise 22**   Convince yourself using pen and paper that ≤ on natural numbers makes a partial order, that is, it satisfies all properties of Definition 7. Afterward, try to understand the proofs for reflexivity, transitivity, and antisymmetry by deducing them yourself in Idris using holes.

5.3. Computations as Types

As stated earlier, types are first-class citizens in Idris. This section shows you how to represent computation at the type level.

5.3.1. Same Elements in a List (Vector)

Reusing the same definition of MyVect, you can write a function to test if all elements are the same in a given list:

```
1  allSame : (xs : MyVect n) -> Bool
2  allSame Empty              = True
3  allSame (Cons x Empty)     = True
4  allSame (Cons x (Cons y xs)) = x == y && allSame xs
```

Idris will return True when all the elements are equal to each other, and False otherwise. Now think about how you can represent this function in terms of types. You want a type called AllSame that has three constructors:

1. AllSameZero is a proof for AllSame in case of an empty list.

2. AllSameOne is a proof for AllSame in case of a single-element list.

3. AllSameMany is a proof for AllSame in case of a list with multiple elements.

This is how the data type could look:

```
1  data AllSame : MyVect n -> Type where
2      AllSameZero : AllSame Empty
3      AllSameOne : (x : Nat) -> AllSame (Cons x Empty)
4      AllSameMany : (x : Nat) -> (y : Nat) -> (ys :
   MyVect _) ->
5          True = (x == y) -> AllSame (Cons y ys) ->
6          AllSame (Cons x (Cons y ys))
```

The AllSameZero and AllSameOne constructors are easy. However, the AllSameMany recursive constructor is a bit trickier. It accepts two natural numbers, x and y, a list ys, a proof that x and y are the same, and a proof that y concatenated to ys is a same-element list. Given this, it will produce a proof that x concatenated to y concatenated to ys is also a same-element list. This type definition captures exactly the definition of a list that would contain all the same elements.

Interacting with the constructors:

```
1  Idris> AllSameZero
2  AllSameZero : AllSame Empty
3  Idris> AllSameOne 1
4  AllSameOne 1 : AllSame (Cons 1 Empty)
5  Idris> AllSameMany 1 1 Empty Refl (AllSameOne 1)
6  AllSameMany 1 1 Empty Refl (AllSameOne 1) : AllSame (Cons 1
7      (Cons 1 Empty))
```

The third example is a proof that the list [1, 1] has the same elements. However, if you try to use the constructor with different elements:

```
1  Idris> AllSameMany 1 2 Empty
2  AllSameMany 1 2 Empty : (True = False) -> AllSame (Cons 2
   Empty) ->
3      AllSame (Cons 1 (Cons 2 Empty))
```

You can see that Idris requires you to provide proof that True = False, which is impossible. For some lists, the AllSame type cannot be constructed, but for others, it can. If you now want to create a function that given a list, maybe produces an AllSame type, you need to consider the Maybe data type first, which has the following definition:

```
1  data Maybe a = Just a | Nothing
```

Interacting with it:

```
1  Idris> the (Maybe Nat) (Just 3)
2  Just 3 : Maybe Nat
3  Idris> the (Maybe Nat) Nothing
4  Nothing : Maybe Nat
```

You can now proceed to write the function:

```
1  mkAllSame : (xs : MyVect n) -> Maybe (AllSame xs)
2  mkAllSame Empty                       = Just AllSameZero
3  mkAllSame (Cons x Empty)                = Just (AllSameOne x)
4  mkAllSame (Cons x (Cons y xs)) with (x == y) proof x_eq_y
5      mkAllSame (Cons x (Cons y xs)) | False =
6          Nothing
7      mkAllSame (Cons x (Cons y xs)) | True =
8          case (mkAllSame (Cons y xs)) of
9              Just y_eq_xs => Just (AllSameMany x y xs
                   x_eq_y y_eq_xs)
10             Nothing      => Nothing
```

Interacting with it:

```
1  Idris> mkAllSame (Cons 1 Empty)
2  Just (AllSameOne 1) : Maybe (AllSame (Cons 1 Empty))
3  Idris> mkAllSame (Cons 1 (Cons 1 Empty))
4  Just (AllSameMany 1 1 Empty Refl (AllSameOne 1)) : Maybe
   (AllSame
5     (Cons 1 (Cons 1 Empty)))
6  Idris> mkAllSame (Cons 1 (Cons 2 Empty))
7  Nothing : Maybe (AllSame (Cons 1 (Cons 2 Empty)))
```

For lists that contain the same elements, it will use the Just constructor, and Nothing otherwise. Finally, you can rewrite the original allSame as follows:

```
1  allSame' : MyVect n -> Bool
2  allSame' xs = case (mkAllSame xs) of
3      Nothing => False
4      Just _ => True
```

5.3.2. Evenness of Numbers

Next, you can represent a data type using a natural deduction style and then do the same corresponding definitions in Idris.

ℹ **Definition 8**   In **natural deduction style,** propositions are represented with a line in the middle, where everything above the line are the premises and everything below it is the conclusion.

When there is an implication ($\rightarrow$) within one of the rules in natural deduction style, this implication is thought to be at the object level, while the actual line represents implication at the metalanguage level. You'll see an example of this in Appendix A.

As an example, let the first inference rule be $\overline{Ev0}$. Note that there is nothing above the line, so you can think of this as an "axiom." Using the previous notation, this would just be $Ev\ 0$. Further, let the second inference rule be $\dfrac{Ev\,n}{Ev(S(Sn))}$ Using the previous notation, this would be $\forall n,\ Ev\ n \rightarrow Ev\ (S\ (S\ n))$.

The same representation in Idris:

```
1  data Ev : Nat -> Type where
2      EvZero : Ev Z
3      EvSucc : (n : Nat) -> Ev n -> Ev (S (S n))
```

Having this definition, you can now construct proofs of even numbers as follows:

```
1  Idris> EvSucc 0 EvZero
2  EvSucc 0 EvZero : Ev 2
3  Idris> EvSucc 2 (EvSucc 0 EvZero)
4  EvSucc 2 (EvSucc 0 EvZero) : Ev 4
```

You just represented even numbers at the type level, where in Section 4.1.4, you represented them at the value level with the even function.

5.4. Trees

A *tree structure* is a way to represent hierarchical data. This section works with *binary* trees, which are trees that contain exactly two sub-trees (nodes). You can define this tree structure using the following implementation:

```
1  data Tree = Leaf | Node Nat Tree Tree
```

This definition states that a tree is defined as one of:

1. Leaf, which has no values.

2. Node, which holds a number and points to two other trees (which can be either Nodes or Leafs).

For example, you can use the Node 2 (Node 1 Leaf Leaf) (Node 3 Leaf Leaf) expression to represent the following tree:

```
1    2
2   / \
3  1   3
```

Edges can be thought of as the number of "links" from a node to its children. Node 2 in this tree has two edges: (2, 1) and (2, 3).

✏️ **Exercise 23**   Come up with a few trees by using these value constructors.

5.4.1. Depth

ℹ️ **Definition 9**   The **depth** of a tree is defined as the number of edges from the node to the root.

You can implement the recursive function depth as follows:

```
1  depth : Tree -> Nat
2  depth Leaf        = 0
3  depth (Node n l r) = 1 + maximum (depth l) (depth r)
```

If you pass a Tree to the depth function, Idris will pattern-match the types and you can extract the values. For example, in the Node case, you pattern-match to extract the sub-trees l and r for further processing. For the Leaf case, since it's just an empty leaf, there are no links to it.

In order to prove that the depth of a tree is greater than or equal to 0, you can approach the proof as follows:

```
1  depth_tree_gt_0 : (tr : Tree) -> GTE (depth tr) 0
2  depth_tree_gt_0 tr = ?prf
```

For the hole, you get:

```
1    tr : Tree
2  -------------------------------------
3  prf : LTE 0 (depth tr)
```

Doesn't seem like you have enough information. You can proceed with proof by cases:

```
1  depth_tree_gt_0 : (tr : Tree) -> GTE (depth tr) 0
2  depth_tree_gt_0 Leaf              = ?prf1
3  depth_tree_gt_0 (Node v tr1 tr2) = ?prf2
```

Check the types of the holes:

```
1  Holes: Main.prf2, Main.prf1
2  Idris> :t prf1
3  --------------------------------------
4  prf1 : LTE 0 0
5  Idris> :t prf2
6    tr1 : Tree
7    tr2 : Tree
8    _t : Nat
9  --------------------------------------
10 prf2 : LTE 0 (S (maximum (depth tr1) (depth tr2)))
```

For the first case, it's pretty easy. You just use the LTEZero constructor with implicit right = 0:

```
1  depth_tree_gt_0 : (tr : Tree) -> GTE (depth tr) 0
2  depth_tree_gt_0 Leaf              = LTEZero {right = 0}
3  depth_tree_gt_0 (Node v tr1 tr2) = ?prf2
```

For the second case, it also seems you need to use LTEZero, but the second argument is (S (maximum (depth tr1) (depth tr2))).

```
1  depth_tree_gt_0 : (tr : Tree) -> GTE (depth tr) 0
2  depth_tree_gt_0 Leaf              =
3      LTEZero {right = 0}
4  depth_tree_gt_0 (Node v tr1 tr2) =
5      LTEZero {right = 1 + maximum (depth tr1) (depth tr2)}
```

Thus, you have proven that the depth of any tree is greater than or equal to 0.

5.4.2. Map and Size

You saw how to use map with lists. It would be neat if you had a way to map trees as well. The following definition allows you to do exactly that:

```
1  map_tree : (Nat -> Nat) -> Tree -> Tree
2  map_tree _ Leaf            = Leaf
3  map_tree f (Node v tr1 tr2) = (Node (f v)
4                                 (map_tree f tr1)
5                                 (map_tree f tr2))
```

The map_tree function accepts a function and a Tree and then returns a modified Tree where the function is applied to all values of the nodes. In the case of Leaf, it just returns Leaf, because there's nothing to map to. In the case of a Node, it returns a new Node whose value is applied to the f function and then recursively maps over the left and right branches of the node. You can use it as follows:

```
1  Idris> Node 2 (Node 1 Leaf Leaf) (Node 3 Leaf Leaf)
2  Node 2 (Node 1 Leaf Leaf) (Node 3 Leaf Leaf) : Tree
3  Idris> map_tree (\x => x + 1) (Node 2 (Node 1 Leaf Leaf)
4      (Node 3 Leaf Leaf))
5  Node 3 (Node 2 Leaf Leaf) (Node 4 Leaf Leaf) : Tree
```

ⓘ Definition 10   The **size** of a tree is defined as the sum of the levels of all nodes.

You will now implement size_tree, which is supposed to return the total count of all nodes in a tree:

```
1  size_tree : Tree -> Nat
2  size_tree Leaf = 0
3  size_tree (Node n l r) = 1 + (size_tree l) + (size_tree r)
```

Try it with a few trees:

```
1  Idris> size_tree Leaf
2  0 : Nat
3  Idris> size_tree (Node 1 Leaf Leaf)
4  1 : Nat
5  Idris> size_tree (Node 1 (Node 2 Leaf Leaf) Leaf)
6  2 : Nat
```

5.4.3. Length of Mapped Trees

Prove that, for a given tree and *any* function f, the size of that tree will be the same as the size of that tree mapped with the function f:

```
1  proof_1 : (tr : Tree) -> (f : Nat -> Nat) ->
2      size_tree tr = size_tree (map_tree f tr)
```

This type definition describes exactly that. You can use proof by cases and pattern matching on tr:

```
1  proof_1 Leaf _            = ?base
2  proof_1 (Node v tr1 tr2) f = ?i_h
```

Check the types of the holes:

```
1  Holes: Main.i_h, Main.base
2  Idris> :t base
3    f : Nat -> Nat
4  --------------------------------------
5  base : 0 = 0
6  Idris> :t i_h
```

```
7   v : Nat
8   tr1 : Tree
9   tr2 : Tree
10  f : Nat -> Nat
11  --------------------------------------
12  i_h: S (plus (size_tree tr1) (size_tree tr2)) =
13     S (plus (size_tree (map_tree f tr1)) (size_tree (map_
       tree f 13  tr2)))
```

For the base case, you just use Refl. However, for the inductive hypothesis, you need to do something different. You can try to apply the proof recursively to tr1 and tr2:

```
1  proof_1 : (tr : Tree) -> (f : Nat -> Nat) ->
2     size_tree tr = size_tree (map_tree f tr)
3  proof_1 Leaf _           = Refl
4  proof_1 (Node v tr1 tr2) f = let IH_1 = proof_1 tr1 f in
5                                let IH_2 = proof_1 tr2 f in
6                                ?conclusion
```

You get to the following proof state at this point:

```
1  Holes: Main.conclusion
2  Idris> :t conclusion
3     v : Nat
4     tr1 : Tree
5     tr2 : Tree
6     f : Nat -> Nat
7     IH_1 : size_tree tr1 = size_tree (map_tree f tr1)
8     IH_2 : size_tree tr2 = size_tree (map_tree f tr2)
9  --------------------------------------
10 conclusion : S (plus (size_tree tr1) (size_tree tr2)) =
11             S (plus (size_tree (map_tree f tr1))
12                 (size_tree (map_tree f tr2)))
```

From here, you can just rewrite the hypothesis:

```
1  proof_1 (Node v tr1 tr2) f = let IH_1 = proof_1 tr1 f in
2                                 let IH_2 = proof_1 tr2 f in
3                                 rewrite IH_1 in
4                                 rewrite IH_2 in
5                                 ?conclusion
```

At this point, if you check the type of conclusion, note that you can just use Refl to finish the proof.

Conclusion

You've seen how powerful types are. They allow you to put additional constraints on values. This helps with reasoning about your programs since a whole class of non-valid programs will not be accepted by the type checker. For example, looking at the following function, you immediately know by its type that it returns a natural number:

```
1  f : Nat -> Nat
2  f _ = 6
```

Note that there are many constructors (proofs) for Nat. For example, you also have f _ = 7. Depending on whether you need 6 or 7 in practice has to be additionally checked. But you're certain that it's a natural number (by the type).

Most programming languages that have a type system have the same expressive power as that of propositional logic (no quantifiers). Dependent types are powerful because they allow programmers to express quantifiers, which increases the power of expressiveness. As a result, you can write any kind of mathematical proofs.

In mathematics, everything has a precise definition. This is also the case with Idris. You have to clearly define your functions and types prior to proving any theorems.

? If Idris proves software correctness, what proves the correctness of Idris?

© Boro Sitnikovski 2023
B. Sitnikovski, *Introduction to Dependent Types with Idris*,
https://doi.org/10.1007/978-1-4842-9259-4

Trusted Computing Base (TCB) can be thought of as the "axioms" of Idris; that is, you choose to trust Idris and the way it rewrites, inserts a new given, and so on.

The most challenging part is to come up with the precise properties (specifications) that you should prove in order to claim correctness for your software.

The beauty of all of this is that almost everything is just about types and finding inhabitants (values) of types.

Further Reading

Halmos, P., *Naive Set Theory*, 1960

Hofstadter, D., *Gödel, Escher, Bach*, 1979

Lipovaca, M., *Learn You a Haskell for Great Good*, 2011

Löh, A., McBride C., Swierstra W., *A Tutorial Implementation of a Dependently Typed Lambda Calculus*, 2010

Martin-Löf, P., *Intuitionistic Type Theory*, 1984

Megill, N., *Metamath*, 1997

Morris, D. W., Morris, J., *Proofs and Concepts*, 2016

Pierce, B., *Logical Foundations*, 2011

Pierce, B., *Types and Programming Languages*, 2002

Sitnikovski, B., *Tutorial Implementation of Hoare Logic in Haskell*, 2021

Smullyan, R., *The Gödelian Puzzle Book*, 2013

The Idris Community, *Programming in Idris: A Tutorial*, 2015

Velleman, J. D., *How to Prove It: A Structured Approach*, 1994

Wadler, P., *Propositions as Types*, 2014

© Boro Sitnikovski 2023
B. Sitnikovski, *Introduction to Dependent Types with Idris*,
https://doi.org/10.1007/978-1-4842-9259-4

119

APPENDIX A

Writing a Simple Type Checker in Haskell

This appendix provides a short introduction to the design of type checkers. It is based on the examples of (and may serve as a good introduction to) the book *Types and Programming Languages*.

A.1. Evaluator

Syntax: The syntax per Backus-Naur form is defined as follows:

```
1  <term> ::= <bool> | <num> | If <bool> Then <expr> Else
   <expr> | <arith>
2  <bool> ::= T | F | IsZero <num>
3  <num>  ::= 0
4  <arith> ::= Succ <num> | Pred <num>
```

For simplicity, the examples represent all of them in a single Term:

```
1  data Term =
2      T
3      | F
4      | 0
5      | IfThenElse Term Term Term
6      | Succ Term
```

© Boro Sitnikovski 2023
B. Sitnikovski, *Introduction to Dependent Types with Idris*,
https://doi.org/10.1007/978-1-4842-9259-4

```
7        | Pred Term
8        | IsZero Term
9        deriving (Show, Eq)
```

Rules of Inference

Name	Rule
E-IfTrue	$$\frac{v_2 \to v_2'}{\text{If T Then } v_2 \text{ Else } v_3 \to v_2'}$$
E-IfFalse	$$\frac{v_3 \to v_3'}{\text{If T Then } v_2 \text{ Else } v_3 \to v_3'}$$
E-If	$$\frac{v_1 \to v_1'}{\text{If } v_1 \text{ Then } v_2 \text{ Else } v_3 \to \text{If } v_1' \text{ Then } v_2 \text{ Else } v_3}$$
E-Succ	$$\frac{v_1 \to v_1'}{\text{Succ } v_1 \to \text{Succ } v_1'}$$
E-PredZero	$$\overline{\text{Pred}\, o \to o}$$
E-PredSucc	$$\overline{\text{Pred}\left(\text{Succ } v\right) \to v}$$
E-Pred	$$\frac{v \to v'}{pred\, v \to pred\, v'}$$
E-IszeroZero	$$\overline{\text{Is Zero } O \to T}$$
E-IszeroSucc	$$\overline{\text{Is Zero }\left(\text{Succ } v\right) \to F}$$
E-IsZero	$$\frac{v \to v'}{\text{Is Zero } v \to \text{Is Zero } v'}$$

Name	Rule
E-Zero	$\overline{O}$
E-True	$\overline{T}$
E-False	$\overline{F}$

Recall that $\dfrac{x}{y}$ can be thought of as the implication $x \rightarrow y$ at the metalanguage level, where the actual arrow $\rightarrow$ is the implication at the object level (in this case, simply eval).

Given these rules, you can reduce terms by pattern-matching them. Implementation in Haskell is mostly "copy-paste" according to the rules:

```
1   eval :: Term -> Term
2   eval (IfThenElse T v2 _) = v2
3   eval (IfThenElse F _ v3) = v3
4   eval (IfThenElse v1 v2 v3) = let v1' = eval v1 in
    IfThenElse v1' v2 v3
5   eval (Succ v1) = let v1' = eval v1 in Succ v1'
6   eval (Pred 0) = 0
7   eval (Pred (Succ v)) = v
8   eval (Pred v) = let v' = eval v in Pred v'
9   eval (IsZero 0) = T
10  eval (IsZero (Succ t)) = F
11  eval (IsZero v) = let v' = eval v in IsZero v'
12  eval T = T
13  eval F = F
14  eval 0 = 0
15  eval _ = error "No rule applies"
```

As an example, evaluating eval `$ Pred $ Succ $ Pred 0`
corresponds to the following inference rules:

```
1                    ----------- E-PredZero
2                    pred 0 -> 0
3                    ----------------------E-Succ
4             succ (pred 0) -> succ 0
5      --------------------------------------E-Pred
6   pred (succ (pred 0)) -> pred (succ 0)
```

A.2. Type Checker

Syntax: In addition to the previous syntax, you can create a new one
for types:

```
1   <type> ::= Bool | Nat
```

In Haskell:

```
1   data Type = TBool | TNat
```

Rules of Inference: Getting a type of a term expects a term and either
returns an error or the type derived:

```
1   typeOf :: Term -> Either String Type
```

Name	Rule
T-True	$\overline{T : T\,Bool}$
T-False	$\overline{F : T\,Bool}$
T-Zero	$\overline{O : T\,Nat}$
T-If	$\dfrac{t_1 : Bool, t_2 : T, t_3 : T}{\text{If } t_1 \text{ Then } t_2 \text{ Else } t_3 : T}$

Name	Rule
T-Succ	$$\dfrac{t : \mathrm{T\,Nat}}{\mathrm{Succ}\ t : \mathrm{T\,Nat}}$$
T-Pred	$$\dfrac{t : \mathrm{T\,Nat}}{\mathrm{Pred}\ t : \mathrm{T\,Nat}}$$
T-IsZero	$$\dfrac{t : \mathrm{T\,Nat}}{\mathrm{Is\,Zero}\ t : \mathrm{T\,Bool}}$$

Code in Haskell:

```
1   typeOf T = Right TBool
2   typeOf F = Right TBool
3   typeOf O = Right TNat
4   typeOf (IfThenElse t1 t2 t3) =
5       case typeOf t1 of
6           Right TBool ->
7               let t2' = typeOf t2
8                   t3' = typeOf t3 in
9                   if t2' == t3'
10                  then t2'
11                  else Left "Types mismatch"
12          _ -> Left "Unsupported type for IfThenElse"
13  typeOf (Succ k) =
14      case typeOf k of
15          Right TNat -> Right TNat
16          _ -> Left "Unsupported type for Succ"
17  typeOf (Pred k) =
18      case typeOf k of
19          Right TNat -> Right TNat
```

```
20              _ -> Left "Unsupported type for Pred"
21  typeOf (IsZero k) =
22      case typeOf k of
23          Right TNat -> Right TBool
24          _ -> Left "Unsupported type for IsZero"
```

Going back to the previous example, you can now "safely" evaluate (by type checking first), depending on the type check results.

A.3. Environments

This simple language supports evaluation and type checking, but does not allow for defining constants. To do that, you need some kind of an environment that will hold information about constants.

```
1  type TyEnv = [(String, Type)] -- Type env
2  type TeEnv = [(String, Term)] -- Term env
```

This example also extends the data type to contain TVar for defining variables, and meanwhile also introduces the Let ... in ... syntax:

```
1  data Term =
2      ...
3      | TVar String
4      | Let String Term Term
```

Here are the rules for variables:

Name	Rule
Add binding	$\dfrac{\Gamma, a:T}{\Gamma\ a:T}$
Retrieve binding	$\dfrac{a:T \in \Gamma}{\Gamma\ a:T}$

Haskell definitions:

```
1  addType :: String -> Type -> TyEnv -> TyEnv
2  addType varname b env = (varname, b) : env
3
4  getTypeFromEnv :: TyEnv -> String -> Maybe Type
5  getTypeFromEnv [] _ = Nothing
6  getTypeFromEnv ((varname', b) : env) varname =
7      if varname' == varname then Just b else getTypeFromEnv
       env varname
```

You have the same exact functions for terms:

```
1  addTerm :: String -> Term -> TeEnv -> TeEnv
2  getTermFromEnv :: TeEnv -> String -> Maybe Term
```

Rules of inference (evaluator): eval' is the same as eval, with the following additions:

1. New parameter (the environment) to support retrieval of values for constants

2. Pattern matching for the new Let ... in ... syntax

```
1  eval' :: TeEnv -> Term -> Term
2  eval' env (TVar v) = case getTermFromEnv env v of
3      Just ty -> ty
4      _        -> error "No var found in env"
5  eval' env (Let v t t') = eval' (addTerm v (eval'
   env t) env) t'
```

Now modify IfThenElse slightly to allow for evaluating variables:

```
1  eval' env (IfThenElse T t2 t3) = eval' env t2
2  eval' env (IfThenElse F t2 t3) = eval' env t3
3  eval' env (IfThenElse t1 t2 t3) =
4     let t' = eval' env t1 in IfThenElse t' t2 t3
```

The remaining definitions can be copy and pasted.

Rules of Inference (Type Checker): typeOf' is the same as typeOf, with the only addition to support env (for retrieval of types for constants in an env) and the new let syntax.

```
1  typeOf' :: TyEnv -> Term -> Either String Type
2  typeOf' env (TVar v) = case getTypeFromEnv env v of
3     Just ty -> Right ty
4     _       -> Left "No type found in env"
5  typeOf' env (Let v t t') = case typeOf' env t of
6     Right ty -> typeOf' (addType v ty env) t'
7     _        -> Left "Unsupported type for Let"
```

For the remaining cases, the pattern-matching clauses need to be updated to pass env where applicable.

To conclude, the evaluator and the type checker almost live in two separate worlds—they do two separate tasks. If you want to ensure the evaluator will produce the correct results, you must first assure that the type checker returns no errors. Another interesting observation is how pattern-matching the data type is similar to the hypothesis part of the inference rules. The relationship is due to the Curry-Howard isomorphism. When you have a formula a ⊢ b (a implies b) and pattern-match on a, it's as if you assumed a and need to show b.

APPENDIX B

Theorem Provers

B.1. Metamath

Metamath is a programming language that can express theorems accompanied by a proof checker. The interesting thing about this language is its simplicity. You start by defining a formal system (variables, symbols, axioms, and rules of inference) and proceed with building new theorems based on the formal system.

As you've seen, proofs in mathematics (and Idris to some degree) are usually done at a very high level. Even though the foundations are formal systems, it is very difficult to do proofs at a low level. However, programming languages like Metamath work at the lowest level, that is formal systems.

The most basic concept in Metamath is the substitution method.[1] Metamath uses an RPN stack[2] to build hypotheses and then rewrites them using the rules of inference in order to reach a conclusion. Metamath has a very simple syntax. A token is a Metamath token if it starts with $, otherwise, it is a user-generated token. Here is a list of Metamath tokens:

- $c defines constants

---

[1] This method makes it easy to follow any proof *mechanically*. However, this is very different from understanding the *meaning* of a proof, which in some cases may take a long time of studying.

[2] Reverse Polish Notation is a mathematical notation where functions follow their arguments. For example, to represent 1 + 2, you would write 1 2 +.

© Boro Sitnikovski 2023
B. Sitnikovski, *Introduction to Dependent Types with Idris*,
https://doi.org/10.1007/978-1-4842-9259-4

- $v defines variables

- $f defines the type of variables (floating hypothesis)

- $e defines required arguments (essential hypotheses)

- $a defines axioms

- $p defines proofs

- $= and $. start and end the body of a proof

- $(and $) start and end the code comments

- ${ and $} start and end the proof blocks

Besides these tokens, there are several rules:

1. A hypothesis is defined by using the $e or $f token.

2. For every variable in $e, $a, or $p, there has to be a $f token defined; that is, any variable in an essential hypothesis/axiom/proof must have defined a type.

3. An expression that contains $f, $e, or $d is active in the given block from the start of the definition until the end of the block. An expression that contains $a or $p is active from the start of the definition until the end of the file.

4. Proof blocks have an effect on the access of definitions, that is, scoping. For a given code in a block, only $a and $p remain visible outside of the block.

The following example defines a formal system and demonstrates the use of the rule *modus ponens* in order to get to a new theorem, based on the initial axioms:

```
1   $( Declaration of constants $)
```

```
 2  $c -> ( ) wff |- I J $.
 3
 4  $( Declaration of variables $)
 5  $v p q $.
 6
 7  $( Properties of variables, i.e. they are well-formed
    formulas $)
 8  wp $f wff p $. $( wp is a "command" we can use in RPN that
    represents a\
 9   well-formed p $)
10  wq $f wff q $.
11
12  $( Modus ponens definition $)
13  ${
14      mp1 $e |- p $.
15      mp2 $e |- ( p -> q ) $.
16      mp $a |- q $.
17  $}
18
19  $( Definition of initial axioms $)
20  wI $a wff I $. $( wI is a "command" that we can use in RPN
    that repres\
21  ents a well-formed I $)
22  wJ $a wff J $.
23  wim $a wff ( p -> q ) $.
```

This example creates constants (strings) ->, wff, and so on, that you
will use in this system. Further, it defines p and q to be variables. The
strings wp and wq specify that p and q are wff (well-formed formulas),
respectively. The definition of modus ponens says that, for a given p (mp1)
and a given $p \rightarrow q$ (mp2), you can conclude q (mp), that is, $p, p \rightarrow q \vdash q$.
Note that outside of this block, only mp is visible per these rules. The initial

axioms state that I, J, and p -> q are well-formed formulas. Separate wff from |-, because otherwise if you just used |-, all of the formulas would be true, which does not make sense.

Having defined the formal system, you can proceed with the proof:

```
1   ${ $( Use block scoping to hide the hypothesis outside of
    the block $)
2       $( Hypothesis: Given I and I -> J $)
3       proof_I $e |- I $.
4       proof_I_imp_J $e |- ( I -> J ) $.
5       $( Goal: Proof that we can conclude J $)
6       proof_J $p |- J $=
7           wI $( Stack: [ 'wff I' ] $)
8           wJ $( Stack: [ 'wff I', 'wff J' ] $)
9           $( We specify wff for I and J before using mp,
            since the types \
10  have to match $)
11          proof_I        $( Stack: [ 'wff I', 'wff J',
            '|- I' ] $)
12          proof_I_imp_J $( Stack: [ 'wff I', 'wff J', '|- I',
            '|- ( I -> \
13  J )' ] $)
14          mp $( Stack: [ '|- J' ] $)
15      $.
16  $}
```

With this code, you assume proof_I and proof_I_imp_J in some scope/context. Further, with proof_J, you want to show that you can conclude J. To start the proof, put I and J on the stack by using the commands wI and wJ. Now that the stack contains ['wff I', 'wff J'], you can use proof_I to use the first parameter from the stack to conclude |- I. Since proof_I_imp_J accepts two parameters, it will use the first two parameters from the stack—that is, wff I and wff J—to conclude |- I -> J. Finally, with mp you use |- I and |- I -> J from the stack to conclude that |- J.

B.2. Simple Theorem Prover

This section puts formal systems into action by building a proof tree generator in Haskell. You should be able to specify axioms and inference rules and then query the program so that it will produce all valid combinations of inference in an attempt to reach the target result.

Start by defining the data structures as follows:

```
1  -- | A rule is a way to change a theorem
2  data Rule a = Rule { name :: String, function :: a -> a }
3  -- | A theorem is consisted of an axiom and list of
   rules applied
4  data Thm a = Thm { axiom :: a, rulesThm :: [Rule a],
   result :: a }
5  -- | Proof system is consisted of axioms and rules
   between them
6  data ThmProver a = ThmProver { axioms :: [Thm a], rules ::
   [Rule a] }
7  -- | An axiom is just a theorem already proven
8  mkAxiom a = Thm a [] a
```

To apply a rule to a theorem, create a new theorem whose result is all the rules applied to the target theorem. You also need a function that will apply all the rules to all the theorems:

```
1  thmApplyRule :: Thm a -> Rule a -> Thm a
2  thmApplyRule thm rule = Thm (axiom thm) (rulesThm thm
   ++ [rule])
```

133

```
3        ((function rule) (result thm))
4
5    thmApplyRules :: ThmProver a -> [Thm a] -> [Thm a]
6    thmApplyRules prover (thm:thms) = map (thmApplyRule thm)
     (rules prover)
7        ++ (thmApplyRules prover thms)
8    thmApplyRules _ _ = []
```

In order to find a proof, search through the theorem results and see if the target is there. If it is, just return. Otherwise, recursively go through the theorems and apply rules in order to attempt to find the target theorem.

```
1    -- | Construct a proof tree by iteratively applying
     theorem rules
2    findProofIter :: (Ord a, Eq a) =>
3        ThmProver a -> a -> Int -> [Thm a] -> Maybe (Thm a)
4    findProofIter _ _ 0 _ = Nothing
5    findProofIter prover target depth foundProofs =
6        case (find (\x -> target == result x) foundProofs) of
7        Just prf -> Just prf
8        Nothing -> let theorems = thmApplyRules prover
           foundProofs
9            proofsSet = fromList (map result foundProofs)
10           theoremsSet = fromList (map result theorems) in
11           -- The case where no new theorems are produced, A
             union B = A
12           if (union proofsSet theoremsSet) == proofsSet
             then Nothing
13           -- Otherwise keep producing new proofs
14           else findProofIter prover target (depth - 1)
15                (mergeProofs foundProofs theorems)
```

Where mergeProofs is a function that merges two lists of theorems, avoiding duplicates. Here's an example:

```
1   muRules = [
2     Rule "One" (\t -> if (isSuffixOf "I" t) then (t ++
      "U") else t)
3     , Rule "Two"    (\t ->
4       case (matchRegex (mkRegex "M(.*)") t) of
5         Just [x] -> t ++ x
6         _         -> t)
7     , Rule "Three" (\t -> subRegex (mkRegex "III") t "U")
8   nn, Rule "Four" (\t -> subRegex (mkRegex "UU") t "")
9     ]
10
11  let testProver = ThmProver (map mkAxiom ["MI"]) muRules in
12    findProofIter testProver "MIUIU" 5 (axioms testProver)
```

As a result, you get that for a starting theorem MI, you apply rule "One" and rule "Two" (in that order) to get to MIUIU (the target proof that you specified).

APPENDIX C

IO, Codegen Targets, Compilation, and FFI

This appendix is most relevant to programmers who have experience with programming languages such as C, Haskell, JavaScript. It demonstrates how Idris can interact with the outside world (IO) and with those programming languages.

In the following examples, you see how to compile Idris code. A given program in Idris can be compiled to a binary executable or a backend for some other programming language. If you decide to compile to a binary executable, the C backend will be used by default.

C.1. IO

IO stands for Input/Output. Writing to a disk file, talking to a network computer, and launching rockets are examples of IO operations.

Functions can be roughly categorized into two parts: **pure** and **impure**.

1. Pure functions produce the same result every time they are called

2. Impure functions might return a different result on a function call

© Boro Sitnikovski 2023
B. Sitnikovski, *Introduction to Dependent Types with Idris*,
https://doi.org/10.1007/978-1-4842-9259-4

An example of a pure function is f(x) = x + 1. An example of an impure function is f(x) = launch x rockets. Since this function causes side-effects, sometimes the launch of the rockets may not be successful (e.g., the case where there are no more rockets to launch).

Computer programs are not usable if there is no interaction with the user. One problem that arises with languages such as Idris (where expressions are mathematical and have no side effects) is that the IO contains side effects. For this reason, such interactions will be encapsulated in a data structure that looks something like this:

```
1  data IO a -- IO operation that returns a value of type a
```

The concrete definition for IO is built within Idris itself, which is why you leave it at the data abstraction, as defined previously. Essentially, IO describes all operations that need to be executed. The resulting operations are executed externally by the Idris Run-Time System (or IRTS). The most basic IO program is:

```
1  main : IO ()
2  main = putStrLn "Hello world"
```

The putStrLn type says that this function receives a String and returns an IO operation.

```
1  Idris> :t putStrLn
2  putStrLn : String -> IO ()
```

You can read from the input similarly:

```
1  getLine : IO String
```

To combine several IO functions, you use the do notation as follows:

```
1  main : IO ()
2  main = do
3      putStr "What's your name? "
```

```
4      name <- getLine
5      putStr "Nice to meet you, "
6      putStrLn name
```

In the REPL, you can use :x main to execute the IO function.
Alternatively, if you save the code to test.idr, you can use the idris
test.idr -o test command to output an executable file that you can use
in your system. Interacting with it:

```
1  boro@boro:~$ idris test.idr -o test
2  boro@boro:~$ ./test
3  What's your name? Boro
4  Nice to meet you, Boro
5  boro@boro:~$
```

Now slightly rewrite this code by abstracting out the concatenation
function:

```
1  concat_string : String -> String -> String
2  concat_string a b = a ++ b
3
4  main : IO ()
5  main = do
6      putStr "What's your name? "
7      name <- getLine
8      let concatenated = concat_string "Nice to meet
       you, " name
9      putStrLn concatenated
```

Note how the let x = y syntax is used with pure functions. In
contrast, you use the x <- y syntax with impure functions.

The ++ operator is a built-in one used to concatenate lists. A String can be viewed as a list of Char. In fact, Idris has functions—called pack and unpack—that allow for conversion between these two data types:

```
1  Idris> unpack "Hello"
2  ['H', 'e', 'l', 'l', 'o'] : List Char
3  Idris> pack ['H', 'e', 'l', 'l', 'o']
4  "Hello" : String
```

C.2. Codegen

The module and import keywords allow you to specify a name of the currently executing code context and load other modules by referring to their names. You can implement your own backend for a given programming language, for which you need to create a so-called *Codegen* (CG) program. An empty CG program looks like this:

```
1  module IRTS.CodegenEmpty(codegenEmpty) where
2
3  import IRTS.CodegenCommon
4
5  codegenEmpty :: CodeGenerator
6  codegenEmpty ci = putStrLn "Not implemented"
```

Since Idris is written in Haskell, the IRTS (Idris Run-Time System) package is a Haskell collection of modules. It contains data structures in which you need to implement Idris commands and give definitions for how they map to the target language. For example, a putStr could map to printf in C.

C.3. Compilation

This section shows how Idris can generate a binary executable and JavaScript code. It also explains the difference between total and partial functions and how Idris handles both cases. Say you define a dependent type Vect, which will allow you to work with lists and additionally have the length of the list at the type level:

```
1  data Vect : Nat -> Type -> Type where
2      VNil : Vect Z a
3      VCons : a -> Vect k a -> Vect (S k) a
```

This code defines Vect as a data structure with two constructors: empty (VNil) or element construction (VCons). An empty vector is of type Vect 0 a, which can be Vect 0 Int, Vect 0 Char, and so on. One example of a vector is VCons 1 VNil : Vect 1 Integer, where a list with a single element is represented; note how the type contains the information about the length of the list. Another example is VCons 1.0 (VCons 2.0 (VCons 3.0 VNil)) : Vect 3 Double.

You will see how total and partial functions can both pass the compile-time checks, but the latter can cause a runtime error.

```
1  --total
2  list_to_vect : List Char -> Vect 2 Char
3  list_to_vect (x :: y :: []) = VCons x (VCons y VNil)
4  --list_to_vect _ = VCons 'a' (VCons 'b' VNil)
5
6  vect_to_list : Vect 2 Char -> List Char
7  vect_to_list (VCons a (VCons b VNil)) = a :: b :: []
8
9  wrapunwrap : String -> String
10 wrapunwrap name = pack (vect_to_list (list_to_vect
   (unpack name)))
```

```
11
12  greet : IO ()
13  greet = do
14      putStr "What is your name? "
15      name <- getLine
16      putStrLn ("Hello " ++ (wrapunwrap name))
17
18  main : IO ()
19  main = do
20      putStrLn "Following greet, enter any number of chars"
21      greet
```

This code defines the list_to_vect and vect_to_list functions, which convert between dependently typed vectors and lists. Further, there is another function that calls these two functions together. Note how the total keyword and the second pattern match are commented out for the purposes of this example. If you now check the values for this partial function:

```
1  Idris> list_to_vect []
2  list_to_vect [] : Vect 2 Char
3  Idris> list_to_vect ['a']
4  list_to_vect ['a'] : Vect 2 Char
5  Idris> list_to_vect ['a','b']
6  list_to_vect 'a' (VCons 'b' VNil) : Vect 2 Char
7  Idris> list_to_vect ['a','b','c']
8  list_to_vect ['a', 'b', 'c'] : Vect 2 Char
```

It is obvious that you only get a value for the test ['a', 'b'] case. Note that, for the remaining cases, the value is not calculated (computed). Let's investigate what happens at runtime:

```
1  Idris> :exec
```

```
2 Following greet, enter any number of chars
3 What is your name? Hello
4 Idris> :exec
5 Following greet, enter any number of chars
6 What is your name? Hi
7 Hello Hi
8 Idris>
```

Idris stopped the process execution. Going one step further, after it's compiled:

```
1  boro@boro:~$ idris --codegen node test.idr -o test.js
2  boro@boro:~$ node test.js
3  Following greet, enter any number of chars
4  What is your name? Hello
5  /Users/boro/test.js:177
6     $cg$7 = new $HC_2_1$Prelude__List__58__58
       _($cg$2.$1, new $HC_2_1$P\
7  relude__List__58__58_($cg$9.$1, $HC_0_0$
   Prelude__List__Nil));
8                                              \
9                      ^
10
11 TypeError: Cannot read property '$1' of undefined
12 ...
13 boro@boro:~$ node test.js
14 Following greet, enter any number of chars
15 What is your name? Hi
16 Hello Hi
```

You get a runtime error from JavaScript. Now do the same with the C backend:

```
1  boro@boro:~$ idris --codegen C test.idr -o test
2  boro@boro:~$ ./test
3  Following greet, enter any number of chars
4  What is your name? Hello
5  Segmentation fault: 11
6  boro@boro:~$ ./test
7  Following greet, enter any number of chars
8  What is your name? Hi
9  Hello Hi
```

This causes a segmentation fault, which is a runtime error. In conclusion, if you use partial functions, you need to run additional checks in the code to cover the cases for potential runtime errors. Alternatively, if you want to take full advantage of the safety that the type system offers, you should define all functions as total.

By defining the list_to_vect function to be total, you specify that every input has to have an output. All the remaining checks are done at compile-time by Idris and, with that, you're guaranteed that all callers of this function satisfy the types.

C.4. Foreign Function Interface

This example introduces the FFI system, which stands for Foreign Function Interface. It allows you to call functions written in other programming languages.

You can define the test.c file as follows:

```
1  #include "test.h"
2
3  int succ(int i) {
```

```
4      return i+1;
5  }
```

Together with test.h:

```
1  int succ(int);
```

Now you can write a program that calls this function as follows:

```
1  module Main
2
3  %include C "test.h"
4  %link C "test.o"
5
6  succ : Int -> IO Int
7  succ x = foreign FFI_C "succ" (Int -> IO Int) x
8
9  main : IO ()
10 main = do x <- succ 1
11     putStrLn ("succ 1 =" ++ show x)
```

This code uses the built-in function foreign, together with the built-in constant FFI_C, which are defined in Idris as follows:

```
1  Idris> :t foreign
2  foreign : (f : FFI) -> ffi_fn f -> (ty : Type) -> {auto fty
   : FTy f [] \
3  ty} -> ty
4  Idris> FFI_C
5  MkFFI C_Types String String : FFI
```

This can be useful if there's a need to use a library that's already written in another programming language. Alternatively, with IRTS, you can export Idris functions to C and call them from C code. You can define test.idr as follows:

```
1  nil : List Int
2  nil = []
3
4  cons : Int -> List Int -> List Int
5  cons x xs = x :: xs
6
7  show' : List Int -> IO String
8  show' xs = do { putStrLn "Ready to show..." ; pure
   (show xs) }
9
10 testList : FFI_Export FFI_C "testHdr.h" []
11 testList = Data (List Int) "ListInt" $ Fun nil "nil" $ Fun
   cons "cons" \
12 $ Fun show' "showList" $ End
```

Running idris test.idr --interface -o test.o will generate two files: test.o (the object file) and testHdr.h (the header file). Now you can input the following code in a file, for example, test_idris.c:

```
1  #include "testHdr.h"
2
3  int main() {
4      VM* vm = idris_vm();
5      ListInt x = cons(vm, 10, cons(vm, 20, nil(vm)));
6      printf("%s\n", showList(vm, x));
7      close_vm(vm);
8  }
```

Now compile and test everything together:

```
1  boro@boro:~$ ${CC:=cc} test_idris.c test.o`${IDRIS:-idris}
   $@ --includ\
2  e``${IDRIS:-idris} $@ --link` -o test
```

146

```
3  boro@boro:~$ ./test
4  Ready to show...
5  [10, 20]
```

Using this approach, you can write verified code in Idris and export its functionality to another programming language.

APPENDIX D

Implementing a Formal System

So far, you have been mostly using a set of formal systems to prove software correctness. This appendix shows how to *both* create and use a formal system in order to prove facts. For that, you use a minimal implementation of Propositional logic, as described in Chapter 2.

Here's the syntax of the formal system expressed in BNF and the code in Idris:

```
1  --prop    ::= P | Q | R | prop brelop prop
2  --brelop ::= "&&" | "->"
3  data Prop = P | Q | R | And Prop Prop | Imp Prop Prop
```

You now have a way to represent some logical formulas, for example, $P \wedge Q$ as And P Q. Further, in this implementation, you also need a way to differentiate between well-formed formulas and theorems, since not all well-formed formulas are theorems. For that, you'll use the Proof data type and a way to extract a proof:

```
1  data Proof a = MkProof a
2  total fromProof : Proof a -> a
3  fromProof (MkProof a) = a
```

© Boro Sitnikovski 2023
B. Sitnikovski, *Introduction to Dependent Types with Idris*,
https://doi.org/10.1007/978-1-4842-9259-4

Note that MkProof (And P Q) ($\vdash P \land Q$) is different from And P Q ($P \land Q$). However, the MkProof constructor mustn't be used directly; proofs should only be constructed given the rules provided next.

```
1  -- A, B |- A /\ B
2  total ruleJoin : Proof Prop -> Proof Prop -> Proof Prop
3  ruleJoin (MkProof x) (MkProof y) = MkProof (And x y)
4  -- A, B |- A
5  total ruleSepL : Proof Prop -> Proof Prop
6  ruleSepL (MkProof (And x y)) = MkProof x
7  ruleSepL x = x
```

Another powerful rule is the *implication rule*. It accepts a non-proven term Prop, whereas other rules accept proven terms; the hypothesis needn't necessarily be true. It only states that "If this hypothesis were a theorem, then that would be a theorem." The second argument is a function (Proof Prop -> Proof Prop) that accepts a Proof and returns a Proof; basically, another rule that will be used to transform the hypothesis x. As a result, it produces the theorem $x \to y(x)$.

```
1  total ruleImplication : Prop -> (Proof Prop -> Proof Prop)
   -> Proof Prop
2  ruleImplication x f = f (MkProof x)
```

For example, you can prove that $\vdash P \land Q \to P \land P$ with ruleImplication (And P Q) (\x => ruleJoin (ruleSepL x) (ruleSepL x)).

In Idris, you get construction of well-formed formulas for free due to algebraic data structures. In some untyped programming languages, such as Python, you can use hashmaps to simulate the types. In the following code, you have to be extra careful with the conditional checks, whereas in Idris it is simpler due to pattern matching.

```
1  def And(x, y): return {'x': x, 'y': y, 'type': 'and'}
2  def Imp(x, y): return {'x': x, 'y': y, 'type': 'imp'}
```

```
3  def MkProof(x): return {'v': x, 'type': 'proof'}
4  def fromProof(x): return x['v'] if isinstance(x, dict) and
   'v' in x els\
5  e None
6  def ruleJoin(x, y):
7    if not isinstance(x, dict) or not isinstance(y, dict) or
     not 'type' i\
8  n x or not 'type' in y or x['type'] != 'proof' or y['type']
   != 'proof':\
9    return None
10   return MkProof(And(fromProof(x), fromProof(y)))
11 def ruleSepL(x):
12   if not isinstance(x, dict) or not 'type' in x or
     x['type'] != 'proof'\
13 : return None
14   wff = fromProof(x)
15   if wff['type'] == 'and': return MkProof(wff['x'])
16   return MkProof(wff)
17 def ruleImplication(x, y): return MkProof(Imp(x,
   fromProof(y(MkProof(x)\
18 )))) if isinstance(x, dict) and 'type' in x and callable(y)
   else None
```

Note how a formal system (Propositional logic) is embedded within a formal system (Idris/Python), and you can reason about it through symbolic manipulation.

Index

Printed in the United States
by Baker & Taylor Publisher Services